ORION PLAIN AND SIMPLE

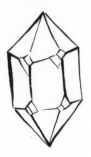

crystals

CASS & JANIE JACKSON

D1438431

Previously published in 2009 as *Simply Crystals* by
Zambezi Publishing Limited, Devon, UK

This edition first published in Great Britain in 2017 by
Orion
an imprint of the Orion Publishing Group Ltd
Carmelite House, 50 Victoria Embankment,
London, EC4Y 0DZ
An Hachette UK Company

*The healing crystals discussed in this book are not recommended as an alternative
to professional medical attention. It is important that if you feel unwell, you should
consult a qualified physician. The crystals we list may aid the healing process and/or
alleviate symptoms, but must on no account be used until accurate medical diagnoses
and appropriate treatment have been given.*

*Crystals and precious gems come from around the world. Find a reputable dealer
when making your purchases, and always check to make sure your crystals and gems
are conflict-free.*

A CIP catalogue record for this book is available
from the British Library.

Paperback ISBN: 978 1 4091 6975 8

eBook ISBN: 978 1 4091 6976 5

Printed and bound by CPI Group (UK), Ltd, Croydon, CR0 4YY

MIX
Paper from
responsible sources
FSC® C104740

www.orionbooks.co.uk

Contents

Crystals

Throughout history, crystals have had a multitude of uses. The earliest use may well have been as decoration—they are, of course, beautiful to behold. But was that all?

Imagine the scene. A stone-age man stoops to pick up from the ground something that glitters and catches his eye. What is it? He carries it home to show his mate. Perhaps they are downcast because he has been unable to find food. However, their sadness is forgotten as they peer at this beautiful crystal. This may have been the beginning of crystal healing. The crystal has, for the moment, healed their worries.

Each time the woman looks at the crystal it lifts her spirits. It was a gift from her partner and she values it, maybe clutching it tightly when he leaves her to go hunting. Perhaps, she thinks, it will ensure that he comes back safely. Later, when he returns, she believes it is because of the crystal. If his hunting has been successful, she will be even more convinced. Was this how crystals first came to be regarded as good luck charms? However these beliefs began, they have increased over the centuries and today are more popular than ever.

Legend has it that crystals were used extensively in Atlantis, where their true value was understood. It is said that the Atlanteans knew how to store information inside a crystal—they were the famous "record keepers" mentioned elsewhere in this book. Yet it is only comparatively recently that we have started to use quartz crystals in modern electronic engineering, and this has enabled us to produce computers on which we now store our records. The Mayans, Hebrews, and Ancient Egyptians employed crystals in their rituals and sacred ceremonies. Today the Australian aborigines still use precious stones and crystals to commune with the spirits.

Over the centuries, through trial and error, certain crystals have been found to produce healing effects of different kinds in varying situations. Only now are we recognizing their vast potential for dealing with physical, emotional, mental, and spiritual problems. Skeptics assert that there is no sound medical evidence for such claims. Even so, thousands of people throughout the world vouch for the extraordinary results they have obtained. It must also be an encouraging thought that eminent scientists and physicians are currently engaged in research on the subject.

Investigation into the use of crystals for divination and for enhancing psychic powers is also ongoing. Obviously such uses cannot yet be claimed as an exact science but crystals have long been utilized as a means of foretelling the future—and who is to say what marvels are yet to be discovered?

In fact, there seem to be as many ways of using these stones as there are types of crystal. This book, admittedly, merely skims the surface of a complex subject but we hope that it will encourage our readers to experiment and investigate further the magic and mystery of crystals.

What Are Crystals?

1

Crystals, in the sense that we use the word here, includes gems, rocks, precious stones, semi-precious stones, or even simply stones. Most crystals are of mineral origin—though modern usage of the term "crystal" includes amber, pearl, coral, and a few items that are not mineral in origin. Some colored stones, such as malachite and rose quartz, are unformed and "rough" when taken from the ground and are usually described as semi-precious. Others, such as the diamond, are equally rough when mined, but are exquisitely cut and polished. Still others, like the amethyst, come out of the ground naturally faceted and already perfect in every way.

Whatever their original forms, crystals have always fascinated mankind because of their beautiful colors or the way they sparkle. Primitive man, recognizing that these stones were different from the soil and rock amongst which they were found, instinctively collected them as something special.

It was then an easy step to endow these beautiful objects with special attributes and magical properties. The Ancient Egyptians believed that crystals could ensure good health, worldly fortune, and protection from evil spirits in this world and the next.

It was the ancient Greeks who gave us the word crystal, derived from *krystallos*, the Greek word that meant both "ice" and "quartz." The ancient Greeks believed that clear quartz was simply ice that had been transmuted into a more permanent state.

The less common a crystal is, the more precious it becomes; thus the diamond is more valuable than the quartz crystal. The larger these crystals are, the less common and even more precious they become. Even today, the largest and most rare stones are found only in royal regalia or in jewelry owned by the extremely wealthy.

As mentioned earlier, this book will list as crystals some materials that are not crystalline in structure. These are nevertheless considered to be gems because of their beauty and rarity. One example is the pearl, which is an organic substance formed by an oyster. Coral, too, is an organic substance, being the external skeleton of tiny marine organisms. Amber is formed by the fossilization of tree resin, and jet is a hard variety of lignite—a close relation to coal.

Most crystals are hard minerals, ranging in color from completely transparent and clear as water—as with the true white diamond and the less expensive crystal Herkimer diamond—through to completely black—as with jet and the crystal known as Apache Tears. Many crystals are homogenous, meaning the whole stone is of uniform color, such as jet. Others are striped, such as sardonyx, or mottled, such as opal. Some crystals, such as tiger's eye, sparkle as they reflect the light from within. Others, such as jasper, are opaque and have only surface color. The variety and intricacy of crystals is endless.

Crystals are all formed in the earth at varying depths, and under varying pressures as well as various temperatures. These factors have a large influence on the type of crystal formed. Some of the types of crystal formation are listed below.

Clusters or beds of crystals are those where a number of crystals grow from the same base. These are capable of healing whole rooms and clearing them of all negative charges.

Single terminated crystals have usually started by being part of a bed and have then been broken off at the base. These crystals are the most easily obtainable and are used for all types of healing. They can vary in size from a few millimeters to over two meters in height.

Double terminated crystals have points on both ends. They can be used in the same way as single terminated crystals but are considered superior to them.

Laser wands are crystals that have grown long and narrow like a wand or knife, usually tapering toward the tip. They are generally clear quartz, though smoky quartz and citrine wands are highly valued. These crystals are particularly effective for healing as their energies flow easily and at great speed, thus having immediate effect.

Twin crystals are exactly what they sound to be: two crystals that have grown together, usually bonded at the base. They are good for balancing the male and female sides of our personalities.

Crystal balls are not found naturally but are cut and polished from a large piece of crystal. They are used for crystal gazing or scrying, and have been used since Ancient Egyptian times for fortune telling. The larger sizes of crystal ball are usually made of glass rather than crystal, so if you want a real crystal one, it will probably have to be fairly small.

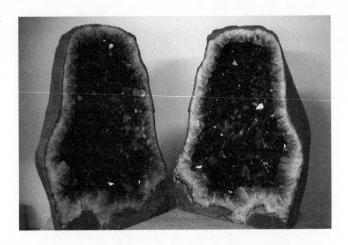

Geodes are not crystals but rounded hollow rocks, commonly the size of a small football. When split open, they display a cluster of crystals lining the inside. These are quite often polished to show the crystals, and some people use them as bookends. Larger geodes, often elongated, are called druses. These are split down the center to show the inside (usually lined with amethyst crystals) and are used for ornamental purposes. These are extremely expensive.

Unformed crystals are seldom cut and facetted. They may be polished but are usually broken into smaller pieces that are then tumbled to produce shiny pebbles. These tumbled stones are the most common and the least expensive. When buying these stones you must insure, by asking, that they have not been artificially treated; the poorer quality stones are often varnished to give them a glossy appearance.

Today, the popularity of crystals and the shortage of good natural specimens means that many broken pieces are now cut, ground, and polished to look like natural terminated stones. They are difficult to identify unless you are quite experienced at looking at crystals, but usually their facets are too perfect, and polished smooth with softened edges, to have been naturally formed. There is nothing wrong with these crystals and they possess as much power as rougher stones, but purists prefer gems as nature made them. If in doubt, ask your retailer.

A natural quartz crystal may have some marks by which it can be identified. Look carefully at the different facets, in a bright light, turning the crystal so that you can see all the different reflections. A natural stone may have some tiny, almost imperceptible marks on its faces that are triangular in shape. These minute surface imperfections, which look as though they have been lightly etched into the crystal, are known as "record keepers," and are much valued. Legend has it that the Atlanteans and Lemurians stored information in quartz crystals and then buried them deep in the earth. It was believed that only those who were capable of decoding the information they contained would then be able to find them. These crystalline libraries of information were supposedly identified by a sacred triangle engraved on their surface. Examine the surfaces of your clear quartz crystals and you may find some of these triangles. They do occasionally appear, mysteriously and inexplicably, on the surface of crystals that previously showed no evidence of them. These precious stones make the very best meditation crystals.

Crystal
Legends and
Folklore

2

Bearing in mind that crystals were known, used and revered for many years before the birth of Christ, it is not surprising that a wide variety of legends and folklore have grown up around them.

Aaron's Breastplate

Perhaps the most famous of these legends concerns the breastplate constructed for Aaron, the first High Priest of Jerusalem. According to the Bible (Exodus 28: 15-20) this breastplate incorporated the use of twelve precious stones (or crystals). These were sardius (carnelian), topaz, carbuncle, emerald, sapphire, diamond, ligure, agate, amethyst, beryl, onyx, and jasper. (*Note that the names of some of the stones used have changed.*) Each stone— thought to measure more than two inches—was to be engraved with the name of one of the twelve tribes of Israel. The very

detailed instructions for the creation of this breastplate indicate that it must have been amazingly beautiful—and extremely heavy.

The Kalpa Tree

The legend of the Kalpa Tree comes from India. Described as an offering to the gods, this "tree" was composed entirely of precious stones, including a trunk made from topaz, diamond, and cat's eye, with sapphire roots, shoots made from emerald, leaves of coral and green zircon, and ruby fruits. This tree was probably the inspiration for the many "crystal trees" currently available in jewelry stores and rock shops.

The New Jerusalem

According to the Bible, the New Jerusalem was built entirely of precious stones. The book of Revelations (21:18-21) says that its walls were made of jasper, streets of gold, and it had twelve gates, each made of a huge pearl. Other stones incorporated in the foundations of the city include jasper, lapis lazuli, chalcedony, emerald, sardonyx, carnelian, peridot, beryl, topaz, chrysoprase, zircon, and amethyst.

Noah's Ark

Some authorities claim that a giant garnet carbuncle, set high up in the center of the boat, illuminated Noah's Ark. Spanish astrologers at one time used the garnet to illustrate the Sun, and, according to the Koran, a carbuncle lights up the fourth heaven.

Crystal Color Folklore

White/Clear Crystals

Small quartz crystals were thought by the Japanese to be the congealed breath of the White Dragon. The Greeks believed that quartz was permanent solidified ice, while aborigines thought it was made of falling stars.

Early Britons gave **quartz** pebbles the name "star stones" and believed them to have healing powers, particularly if they were collected from a stream or running brook.

An ancient Indian legend suggests that **pearls** were dewdrops that fell from heaven and were caught by shellfish. The Arabs shared this belief, claiming that this event occurred in April, while the Hebrews thought that pearls were the tears shed by Eve when she was expelled from the Garden of Eden.

Purple Crystals

Greek legend has it that the god Bacchus was annoyed with mortals and vowed to have the next human he encountered torn apart by his tigers. En route to pray at the temple of Diana, the young girl Amethyst was the next mortal Bacchus met. When the girl screamed to Diana to protect her, the goddess turned her into a pillar of quartz. Overcome by remorse, Bacchus poured a libation of wine over the stone—thus producing the purple color by which **amethyst** is traditionally known.

Lepidolite is known as the peace stone and is said to provide the owner with a guardian angel. It is thought to have a particularly strengthening effect on women.

Red Crystals

Red stones are sometimes considered to possess particularly strong powers. Star **rubies**—that is, crystals with inclusions forming the shape of a star—are particularly venerated in the Orient. The spirits attuned to the star have names that translate as Faith, Hope, and Destiny and are thought to bring good fortune to the owner of the stone.

Blue Crystals

Lapis lazuli was regarded by the Ancient Egyptians and the Sumerians as the Stone of Heaven and sacred to the gods. The hair of the god Ra was said to be composed of the crystal. In Christianity the stone was used to symbolize the purity of the Virgin Mary. It was also believed that when God gave the Ten Commandments to Moses they were written on tablets of this blue, gold-flecked stone.

A cardinal's ring is always a **sapphire**, as decreed by Pope Innocent III, because "this stone possesses qualities essential to its dignified position as the badge of Pontifical Rank and a Seal of Secrets." Solomon was thought to use the stone as a means of communicating with God. It is probable that many references to sapphire in ancient texts are actually referring to lapis lazuli.

Green Crystals

There are innumerable green crystals, but **jade** has always been regarded as one of the most precious. In fact, this crystal comes in a wide variety of colors but it usually identified with green. The stone has been used in China since Neolithic times and was believed to be the solidified semen of a dragon. In South America, jade was sacred to the goddess of storms, Chalchihuitlicue, while the Aztecs and Mayans used it for funeral masks.

In ancient cultures, **peridot** was often mistakenly regarded as an emerald. It has always been used for making amulets and talismans and was thought to be effective in turning around difficult situations. Early Christians regarded it as the stone of the Apostle Bartholomew, representing truth and miracles.

Pink Crystals

Rose quartz has always been regarded as a gentle stone, producing tranquility, love, and reconciliation. It is known to have been in use since at least 2500 BC. The Romans and Egyptians used powdered rose quartz in cosmetics in the belief that it could prevent wrinkles and produce a flawless complexion.

Rhodochrosite was treasured by the Incas because they believed that it contained the blood of their ancestral rulers. For this reason, it is sometimes known as the Inca rose. It is said to hold the power of Venus and to strengthen the ties of love.

Yellow Crystals

Citrine was at one time the blanket description for all yellow stones. It has also been known as Brazilian topaz, false topaz, and a variety of similar names. Legend has it that this crystal was used on Atlantis as a powerful healing tool, particularly connected with the sun. In fact, the citrine is often known as the sunstone and is known to reject any form of negativity.

Norsemen and Vikings believed that **amber** was formed from the tears of the goddess Freya, when Odin left her to travel the world. The Greeks had similar beliefs, but their claim was that amber represented the tears of the Heliades when Zeus has turned their brother Phaeton into a poplar tree. Yet another tearful explanation for this crystal came from India where it is thought to be the fossilized tears of birds. The ancient Romans had other ideas, believing that amber was formed from lynx urine—though Sudine, writing in 240 BC, referred to amber coming from a lynx tree.

Orange Crystals

In Ancient Egypt, the **carnelian**—known as the "Blood of Isis"—was thought to provide protection during astral travel. This was achieved by staring into the crystal after placing it in front of a lighted candle. Placed on the throat of a mummy, a carnelian amulet engraved with the 156th chapter of the Book of the Dead was said to ensure rebirth into the after-life. The famous "Eye of Horus" carnelian amulet, said to offer protection against the evil eye, is still popular in many parts of the Middle East.

Brown Crystals

Tiger's eye was used in Ancient Egypt in at least 3000 BC and was sacred to Ra, the sun god. It was also used as eyes in the statues of various Egyptian and Assyrian gods. The Egyptians believed that this crystal enabled the owner to see anything and everything, even through walls and behind closed doors. Roman soldiers carried it into battle to ensure their courage. In Japan, it was thought to guarantee longevity, as the tiger was supposed to live for 1,000 years. The Indian belief was that tiger's eye created wealth and prevented the wearer from losing money.

Smoky quartz has long been believed to be a protection against bad luck, particularly in the Alpine regions. It can still be found carved into the shape of a cross and hung on bedroom walls to repel evil. This particular form of quartz is said to help the wearer cope with problems and negative situations.

Black Crystals

In South America, both the Aztecs and the Maya regarded **obsidian** as sacred. The Aztec's sacrificial knife was made from this stone and it was regarded as the bringer of life and death. The

Mayans often used this crystal to make magic mirrors consecrated to the god Tezcatlipoca. John Dee, the English Elizabethan seer, is reputed to have had a similar mirror. In North-Central California, boys and girls endured an initiation ceremony, which included being stabbed with

obsidian knives. The crystals known as Apache Tears are actually obsidian; the name originated with the belief that the earth wept whenever an Apache warrior was killed.

Sardonyx was used in India and Persia to protect against the evil eye, in addition to making the wearer invisible if the stone was carved in a particular style. In Christianity the crystal symbolized the Apostles James and Philip, representing their honesty and sincerity. For the Romans, sardonyx was sacred to Mars, the god of war. In the Middle Ages it was worn to protect against grief and to increase confidence. According to St. Hildegard, the devil hated the purity of the sardonyx and would flee from it.

These are but a selection of the many myths and legends that have become associated with crystals over the years. We hope these brief accounts will encourage you to investigate further. It is a fascinating study.

How to Bring Crystals Into Your Life

3

Crystals can have many uses, but most often are used for healing, meditation, divination, and protection. How do you know which ones are right for you? This chapter will teach you how to choose, cleanse, purify, charge, and store your crystal—all of which will help you bind with your crystal, making it uniquely yours.

Choosing Your Crystal

Be prepared to devote a fair amount of time and thought to the selection of your own personal crystal. Realize, first of all, that your body possesses natural vibrations. Crystals, too, vibrate at certain frequencies. Your aim, therefore, is to find a crystal that shares the vibrational rate of your own body. This may sound difficult. In fact, it's a simple and enjoyable task, though it must be done with care.

The first step is to decide on your requirements. Throughout this book (particularly chapters 5 through 8) you will find details of a wide variety of stones, their unique qualities, and the needs with which they are associated. Before you go any further in selecting a crystal, check on the information given here. Then, having found a number of stones that seem appropriate, decide on those which most appeal to you.

Your next step is to go to a rock shop. It's really almost essential to do this, even if you have to travel some distance to find the necessary retailer. Mail-order companies abound and are convenient, but in our view the *only* way to select a crystal is to visit a shop and be in the physical presence of a stone in order to take your pick.

You'll also be able to get help and advice from the shop's staff. They should be able to offer guidance on the quality of the crystals they are selling and answer any questions you may have.

Most important of all, you will be able to hold the crystals in your hands. This is crucial. It is the only way to find out which one is right for you.

On entering the shop, you will probably be bewildered and enchanted by the glittering display of color. Take your time. Stroll around and look carefully at all the stones on display. Almost certainly, you will find that some—perhaps half a dozen—attract you more than the others. Ask if you may examine these more closely. Don't worry, the staff will be accustomed to such requests and will know what you're doing.

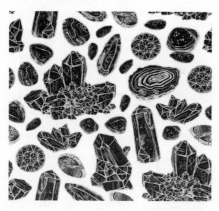

Take each crystal in turn and hold it in your hand for a moment. Close your eyes and take a slow, deep breath. Feel the crystal—its texture, shape, and temperature. Does it "speak" to you? Note your reactions to the crystal before putting it down, picking up another, and repeating the process.

Out of the six or so crystals that you are drawn to, you will probably find a couple that feel "right." At this stage that "rightness" is indefinable, but you'll know it when you feel it. Pause for a little walk around the shop or chat with the staff, and then repeat the above routine with each of the two remaining crystals. This time, you will almost certainly be confident about which is "your" crystal.

The size and quality of a crystal have no effect upon its potency. Naturally, you'll want to buy the biggest and best that you can afford, but don't let this influence your choice. It doesn't matter in the least if "your" crystal is not as big and shiny as some of the others.

Trust your own instincts. When you somehow "recognize" a crystal, don't hesitate and dither about with others. Pay up, ask the shopkeeper to wrap the stone, and carry it home in triumph. You're right at the beginning of a beautiful friendship!

Let the Buyer Beware!

Beware of fake stones or those that have been treated, irradiated, or dyed in order to enhance their color. You want a crystal exactly as nature made it and just as it came out of the ground. Reputable dealers won't try to fob you off with fakes. Don't be afraid to ask if you are holding a genuine, untreated stone. If the seller says that it may have been heat-treated—as smoky quartz, for example, often is—ask if he has any untreated stones. If not, move on to another dealer.

Consider only those stones that you know by name. Don't buy a crystal you've never heard of merely because it looks pretty. There are many synthetic stones on the market, usually with glamorous names. No matter how attractive they look, these are not genuine crystals and are useless for healing, protection, or any other requirement.

Gifts

When your friends hear of your interest in crystals they may buy them for you as gifts. This need not be a problem. Accept the gift graciously, but take particular care with the cleansing and charging of this stone. Cherish it. It was chosen *for* you, rather than *by* you. It may take a little longer for you to "tune in" to one another, but eventually this crystal can be "yours" just as much as one that you have selected yourself.

Hands Off!

When you've found "your" crystal remember that it is not a toy to be played with and passed around for others to handle. You chose it as a working tool and should treasure it as such. Remember, though, that it had probably been handled by lots of people before you made your purchase. The next step is to carefully cleanse your crystal to remove the negative energies that it has collected before it came into your possession. This cleansing process will also personalize your crystal and tune it in to your energy fields.

Cleansing Your Crystal

First you will need to make sure that your crystal is physically clean.

The simplest and easiest method is to clean your crystal under lukewarm running water with a soft toothbrush and a mild, detergent-free soap. When it is clean and sparkling, give it a final rinse using fresh rainwater, spring-water, or filtered water, if at all possible. Then pat it dry with a soft towel. Some prefer to dry their crystal by blowing it gently with their own breath. This is an excellent method as it helps to impart your energies to the crystal.

We recommend you use this method first. Another method is to place your crystal in cold running water for five minutes, or simply leave the stone in a container of rainwater overnight.

Purifying Your Crystal.

There are a wide variety of methods for removing negative vibrations from you crystal, all of which are equally effective.

Bury it in a container of sea-salt. Leave it there for anything between 24 hours and three days. Then remove it from the salt, rinse and dry it as above. Alternatively, dissolve some salt in enough lukewarm water to cover your crystal and proceed as above.

Another method is to leave the stone for at least 36 hours in a container of seawater—but do be sure that this water is not polluted.

Yet another cleansing method is to bury your crystal in moist sand or soil for at least 24 hours.

Note: *Lapis lazuli, malachite, and sodalite can be damaged by water and should therefore not be subjected to any of these methods.*

Smudging is the method of crystal cleansing used by Native Americans. Cedar, sage leaves, and sweetgrass are burned in an open container and the crystal is passed several times through the smoke. New Age shops sell smudge sticks that are a combination of these leaves with other herbs and frankincense. These can be used for cleansing your crystal, your home—and even yourself.

If you are unable to obtain the ingredients for smudging, you can use the smoke from an incense stick or pass your crystal through a candle flame. Be careful not to burn yourself, or damage the crystal by overheating it.

If your climate permits, place your crystal outdoors in the sunlight. Leave it there all day, turning it occasionally so that all its facets catch the sunlight. Beware of magpies and other birds that may be attracted by its glitter and steal it. All crystals are formed beneath the ground and some may be damaged by direct sunlight, which tends to make the colors fade. Those that are at risk are aventurine, amethyst, apatite, and aquamarine, some colors of beryl, celestine, citrine, fluorite, rose quartz, smoky quartz, kunzite, and sapphire.

Some stones cleanse better with moonlight. As above, leave your crystal outdoors on a moonlit night. This may take several nights to work effectively, but is well suited to those crystals listed above that are at risk from sunlight. You can speed up this process by placing your crystal on a mirror, thus doubling the effect of the moon's rays.

All these cleansing and purifying methods work well, but there is one other that is the easiest of all. Simply place your crystal on a crystal cluster that has already been purified and leave it there for no less than 24 hours.

Bonding

The next step in the process of making your crystal into a powerful working tool is to bond with it. This step, although important, may be one that you have taken without realizing it. All you have to do is sit quietly with your crystal in your hands and close your eyes. Then notice the shape, texture and temperature of the crystal, just as you did when buying it. Do this for no more than a couple of minutes. Then open your eyes and examine your crystal minutely, taking in its outward appearance, color, every angle and any flaws or impurities that it may have. Close your eyes again and now, while still holding it, visualize your crystal. See it in your mind's eye. Imprint its appearance on your brain so strongly that at any time in the future you will be able to distinguish it from any other crystal.

Charging

Finally we come to the most important step. This is known as charging or programming your crystal. For example, perhaps you have bought a beautiful piece of citrine in the hope that it will relieve the stress you have been experiencing. You must now empower that crystal so that it will help to stabilize your emotions and create happiness and tranquility in your life.

Your crystal has been cleansed and purified. It is now like a clean slate, waiting to be written on. Sit quietly. Hold your crystal between both hands so that you are making as much contact with it as possible. Close your eyes, relax, and breathe deeply and slowly. Inhale through your nose and exhale in a sharp puff from your mouth. Think of the energy you wish to impart to your crystal. Focus on that intent. Visualize your intentions flowing smoothly from your mind into the crystal. Your thoughts have energy. In this process, you are putting that energy into your crystal. When you inhale, take into your body the image of what it is you want from your crystal. With each exhalation, imagine that desire entering the stone.

This procedure will program the crystal with whatever quality you want. Your vibrations are stored in the crystal, ready to use.

Note: If you use your crystal frequently you will need to recharge it every two or three weeks if you wish to change the purpose for which you use your crystal—citrine may be used to attract wealth—it must first be cleansed and then reprogrammed.

Keep your charged crystal safely where other people will not see or touch it. Crystals that are not being used may be stored on a soft bed of tissue in a drawer, so that they are out of the light. If you wish to carry your crystals with you, the best way is to wear them round your neck in a small pouch. Most rock-shops sell these.

Crystals
for Psychic
Development
and Divination

4

Crystals are a most effective aid to psychic development, concentrating the mind, dispelling negative thoughts, and enhancing spiritual awareness. All types of crystals have also long been used for divination—the most common being the clear quartz crystal ball, regularly used by clairvoyants for fortune telling. Other crystals can also be effective for development, for foretelling the future, and for looking into past lives. The most common are listed below.

Amethyst, which is used universally for healing purposes, can also help to increase psychic awareness. An amethyst crystal stored with any other divinatory stones will enhance their powers.

Clear Quartz in any form may be used as an aid to divination. However, the crystal ball has long been the chosen tool for those who wish to enhance their ability to see into the future. Quartz may also be used for establishing a link with spirit guides and helpful angels. Psychics also use clear quartz crystals to connect with the Akashic records—the Universal Source of Knowledge. This stone is also thought to assist the development of Extra Sensory Perception (ESP).

Hematite enables the user to disconnect from everyday material affairs so that they may then connect with the unseen and develop great psychic powers.

Red Jasper is a very powerful stone to use for predictive purposes. Its most common use is to protect the wearer during out of the body experiences.

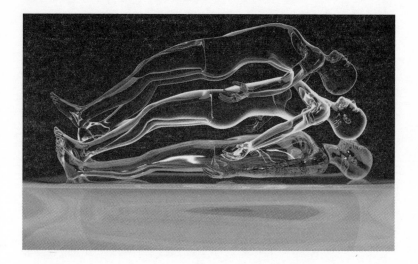

Malachite is used to enhance predictive techniques. It is most helpful when the wearer is seeking information about events in the near future.

Snow Flake Obsidian helps the psychic to dissociate from the physical world and enter into spiritual realms.

Tiger's Eye may be used as a divinatory crystal for those who wish to inquire about their lives in the past or the future.

Although **Calcite** is not a divinatory stone, psychic practitioners and clairvoyants use it for spiritual protection. They also use it to clear the mind before practicing divination.

Psychic Development

There are three methods of using crystals for psychic development. Before you begin, and whichever method you choose, ensure that your crystal is cleansed by you and programmed for you. It is advisable, too, to keep the chosen crystal solely for psychic development, and not use it for other purposes.

1 Seat yourself comfortably with your chosen, cleansed and programmed crystal in you hands. Close your eyes and relax. Let your mind dwell on what you are doing—seeking psychic development for which you need help and guidance. When you feel completely relaxed, open your eyes and stare into your crystal. Feel the energy flowing from your crystal into your mind. If this becomes overpowering, close your eyes and allow that energy be completely absorbed before once again opening your eyes and concentrating on your crystal. As you tune in to your higher self, unusual thoughts may come into your mind, seemingly from nowhere. When you feel that you have absorbed sufficient energy on this occasion put your crystal aside. Close your eyes again, relax, and ground yourself by ensuring that your feet are flat on the ground. Then make notes of any thoughts that came into your mind. At first, these thoughts may not make any sense to you but with time, practice, and patience you will find them gradually coming together, rather like the pieces of a jigsaw.

2 For the second method, you will need to be sure that you will not be interrupted for some time. Lie down on your back with your face upward. Place your cleansed and programmed crystal on the third eye—that is, between and slightly above your two eyebrows.

Close your eyes and relax. Ask for guidance toward the psychic development that you seek. Feel your mind tuning in to your higher self and the energy flowing from the crystal into your mind. This method will produce quicker and more dramatic effects than the first one. The energies will probably manifest as flashing lights and this may prove too much for you to cope with at first. Don't worry. This is quite normal. Simply remove the crystal, relax for a while, and then try again. You may have strange thoughts, as with the first method, but you may also experience visions that flash before your (closed) eyes. When you have finished the session, open your eyes, put your crystal aside, ground yourself again by sitting or standing up with your feet on the ground. Make notes of what you have experienced as for the first method.

This third method is similar to method 2. The only difference is that you will need several charged crystals rather than only one. Lie on your back as before, and place the crystals on the floor in an arc round your head and quite close to it. The advantage of using this method is that you can employ a psychic development crystal, together with a divinatory crystal, and a disconnecting crystal. This method is extremely powerful and you should not practice this technique until you have seen what one crystal can do for you. Whenever you are working with crystals, try to remain calm and relaxed, and don't attempt to hurry anything.

If, after several sessions, you don't receive any significant messages or visions, don't despair. Continue to practice at regular intervals. You will build up your attunement to your higher self and psychic development will follow.

Scrying

If you wish to practice divination by scrying (crystal gazing) the method is very similar to the first psychic development exercise.

Seat yourself comfortably with your chosen, cleansed, and programmed crystal in front of you, preferably on a black background. A piece of black velvet is ideal. Clear crystal quartz is the best crystal for scrying, and if you can get a quartz crystal ball, that will be even better.

Close your eyes and relax. Let your mind dwell on what you are doing, then request help and guidance. Concentrate on what it is you wish to see—your future self, someone else, or perhaps what is happening somewhere else. When your desire is firmly centered in your mind and you feel completely at ease, open your eyes and stare into your crystal. Allow any random thoughts to drift into and out of your mind. Concentrate on your crystal and what you are doing. Feel the energy flowing from your crystal into your mind. Keep your eyes open and try to gaze, unblinking, into and through your crystal.

This method demands time and patience. At first you may see only cloudiness but eventually the clouds may part and you will view whatever it is you are seeking. When you feel that you have finished this session, close your eyes, relax and ground yourself. Make notes of any images that you saw. As previously, these may not make sense to you on the first few occasions, but with practice you will be able to concentrate for longer periods and obtain clearer pictures that are genuinely meaningful. As stated previously, patience, practice, and persistence are vital.

When practicing psychic development or scrying, it is vital to cleanse and re-charge your crystals regularly.

It is also vital to learn to close your chakras after doing such work or you will be too open to unwanted influences. For this and all things psychic, buy *Psychic Plain and Simple* by Ann Caulfield and *Develop Your ESP* by Nina Ashby.

Pendulums

Yet another method of divination uses a crystal pendulum. These can be obtained from rock shops and they consist of a suitable crystal point secured to the end of a chain or thread. Use the same care in choosing your pendulum as you did when selecting your first crystal.

A simple method for using a pendulum is given below, but if you want to explore this field more fully there are books available on the subject. You may also find more information in books about dowsing.

As always, cleanse and charge your crystal before you use it.

Attuning to Your Pendulum

The easiest way to become attuned to your pendulum is to ask it simple questions. Sit at a desk or table so that your elbow is supported, with space for your pendulum to swing in all directions in front of you. Adjust the length of the chain or thread so that the crystal hangs somewhere level with your midriff. Relax and let the crystal slowly come to rest above the table. Be careful to remain completely still so that you do not inadvertently influence the swing of the pendulum.

Now ask your pendulum questions to which you already know the answer. Keep these as simple as possible and ensure that the question can be answered by "yes" or "no."

Try a simple experiment. Suppose that you conduct this trial on a Monday. Ask your pendulum "Is today Tuesday?" Your pendulum may start to slowly rotate counter-clockwise. Make a mental note of the direction. Now hold your pendulum in your other hand and ask "Is today Wednesday?" Again it may rotate counter-clockwise. Make a mental note of this. Next, still your pendulum, then ask "Is today Monday?" This time it will probably rotate in a clockwise direction. You have now established that a clockwise rotation indicates "true" and counter-clockwise represents "false."

Practice with your pendulum in this way until you obtain reliable results regularly. Once this happens, you have attuned to your pendulum and may begin answering questions through this divinatory method.

Always begin each pendulum session by checking out the rotation on known answers. You cannot assume that the original rotation established will be maintained indefinitely.

Crystals for Visualization and Positive Thought

5

Many people use crystals as a focus for visualization and positive thought, believing that this will attract to them the specific benefit they require. Should you wish to adopt this technique, your first step must be to decide on what you need from the stone. It is important to be extremely clear and specific about your aim.

The next step is to find a crystal possessing the appropriate attributes. Consult the list below to make your selection.

Never forget the importance of cleansing and programming your chosen crystal according to your desires. As stated above, it is vital that you are decisive and precise about this. Wear the crystal constantly, as near to your body as possible, until you achieve the benefit you have asked for.

When using a crystal in this way, it is important to cleanse and re-charge it regularly, in order to obtain the maximum benefit.

How Crystals Can Help You

Agate, Banded
Will help you to feel grounded and remain focused, dispelling fears of all kinds.

Agate, Blue lace
Helps you to adjust when one situation is finished and another is about to start. Will enable you to express your views lovingly.

Agate, Moss
Brings peace of mind and refreshes the spirit. Helps to develop intuition.

Agate, Tree

Aids meditation and clear thinking. Helps to relieve stress.

Amazonite

Soothes the nervous system. Helps to increase self-esteem and self-confidence.

Amber

Relieves depression and will lift your spirits if you are unhappy.

Amethyst

The great healer of mind, body, and spirit. Clears the mind, helps develop the intuition and psychic abilities.

Apache Tears

This is a variety of obsidian. It is considered to be an extremely powerful stone for bringing good fortune and will help you to feel more positive.

Apatite

This is a splendid motivator that will aid your communicative powers.

Aquamarine

Meaning "water and the sea," this stone will help you safely navigate the rough seas of life. It promotes compassion and empathy.

Aventurine, Green

Brings good fortune and increases creativity. Heals wounded emotions.

Azurite

Will help you to relinquish harmful beliefs and see the true purpose of life.

Bloodstone

Also known as **heliotrope**. Will help to calm fears, dispel confusion, and rid you of obsessive ideas.

Calcite

This is a great energizer, useful for aiding the fortunate outcome of a new project. It provides excellent psychic protection.

Carnelian

Also known as **sard**, this crystal banishes jealousy and inspires courage. Aids perception and helps when decisions have to be made.

Celestine

Creates a peaceful and serene outlook, and helps you to communicate more effectively.

Chalcedony

Lifts the spirits and helps to balance your emotions.

Chrysocolla

Eases all forms of stress, promotes self-confidence, and helps to balance your emotions.

Chrysolite

A variety of **chrysoberyl**. Also known as **olivine** and **peridot**.

Increases happiness and attracts abundance. Heals old mental wounds. **Alexandrite** is another variety of this stone.

Chrysoprase

Good for relieving stress and tension of all kinds and for spiritual protection. Helps to heal psychological scars.

Citrine

Helps to calm the emotions and instill self-confidence. An inspirational stone that also boosts feelings of self-worth.

Coral

Strengthens and protects the emotions.

Diamond

Great for helping you to see things more clearly and in assisting connection with the infinite.

Emerald

A strong healer of both mental and physical problems.

Fluorite

Helps the individual to become more analytical and rational. Also combats anxiety and worry.

Garnet

Known as **carbuncle** when cut as a cabochon. Useful as a protector against depression and melancholy, this crystal also encourages patience and perseverance.

Hematite

Aids psychic development and helps to overcome shyness and build self-esteem.

Jade

A useful healing stone, encouraging longevity and healing both body and spirit. It brings good luck and friendships.

Jasper

A stress reliever that is useful for grounding those who practice divination. Promotes tranquility.

Jet

Helps to keep evil spirits at bay, strengthens the character and helps you to be resolute in the face of adversity.

Kunzite

Helps to align the emotions rationally. Relieves emotional stress and provides serenity.

Labradorite

Helps develop strong psychic powers.

Lapis Lazuli

Aids visualization and helps develop the sixth sense. Stimulates the intuition and promotes creativity.

Lepidolite

Great for relieving stress and dispelling negative emotions.

Malachite

A great healer, particularly for dealing with negative and repressed emotions.

Moonstone

Restores harmony and emotional balance wherever they may be lacking.

Mother of Pearl

Helps the wearer to accept love.

Obsidian

Can be used as a scrying stone. Helps the user to focus on the paranormal.

Onyx

Establishes a protective psychic shield around the wearer. Enhances emotional stability.

Opal

Helps the wearer rationalize emotional states and see all the possibilities in a given situation.

Pearl

Enhances feelings of self-respect. Aids self-esteem and stability.

Pyrite

Opens the mind to accept new ideas.

Quartz, Clear

"The mirror of the soul." A great tool as an aid to channeling and helping meditation. A powerful healer that stores and transmits energy.

Quartz, Rose

Attracts and teaches love in its widest, most universal sense. Gives comfort and relieves grief. Promotes harmonious relationships.

Quartz, Rutilated

Releases energy blockages and improves self-esteem.

Quartz, Smoky

Filters out negative thoughts and emotions. Helps with telepathy and universal communication.

Rhodonite

Aids self-esteem, assurance, and confidence.

Rhotochrisite

Balances the emotions, especially where love is concerned. Promotes understanding.

Ruby

Helps the wearer to be realistic about aims and ambitions. Purifies love. Promotes spiritual knowledge.

Sapphire

A great aid to mental clarity, clearing the inner eye, and bringing good fortune to the wearer.

Sodalite

Useful for healing damaged emotions. Helps the wearer to think rationally. Aids restful sleep.

Spinel

"The mother of ruby" protects the wearer from emotional upset.

Sugulite

A great aid to spiritual insight and for attaining tranquility.

Tanzanite

Helps the wearer to accept change.

Tiger's Eye

Protects the wearer. Also, a useful aid for those seeking knowledge of past or future lives. Promotes patience and persistence.

Topaz

Allows the wearer to transmit their visualizations as universal messages. An aid to telepathy. Useful for artists.

Tourmaline, Black

Repels all negative energies and protects the wearer from destructive forces.

Tourmaline, Green

Useful for bringing abundance and for helping with creative endeavors.

Tourmaline, Pink

A feminine stone, useful for women. Strengthens and harmonizes the female sexual organs. Also helps men to discover their feminine side.

Turquoise

A great aid for drawing luck, love and money to the wearer and bringing emotional balance.

Unakite

Helps to heal the psyche and allows the wearer to recognize the higher self.

Zircon

An invigorating stone that enhances creativity and originality.

Crystals for Meditation

6

Traditionally, meditation has been used to enhance spiritual growth but today it is equally popular as a means of relaxation and stress management. It works by slowing down the physical processes and allowing the mind to become as relaxed as the body. The popular belief that meditation requires you to completely empty your mind is incorrect. Most people would find this impossible. A more accurate description is that meditation is a method of focusing the mind in such a way that the inner "chatter" is stilled.

In the frenetic world of the 21st century, this can prove difficult. Newcomers to meditation invariably require a tangible object on which to concentrate. This can be almost anything; a candle flame, a flower—or a crystal. Crystals focus your energy by raising your vibrations. This in turn, enables you to concentrate more easily.

There is an easy method for using a crystal in meditation. Simply hold the crystal in one hand or between your palms. If you prefer, place the crystal on a table or stool and sit in front of it. This is probably the best method if you are using a large stone. For a successful meditation you need to be calm and be prepared to open yourself up to the crystal energy. Relax and try to let go of the outside world.

Sit quietly in a comfortable position at a time when you know that you are not going to be disturbed. Simply gaze at your crystal, relax and open yourself up to the energy from the stone. Breathe regularly and evenly. Concentrate on the crystal and the vibrations coming from it.

Don't struggle to make your mind a blank. Allow your thoughts to drift (as they certainly will) but, whenever your mind wanders, gently return the focus to your crystal and what you want from it. Remember that meditation is about listening. Listen to what the crystal has to tell you. Think your specific desire into your crystal and then wait for an answer. It will come, in its own good time.

Don't try to rush things or try to hurry the meditation along. It doesn't matter if you don't get an immediate response to your wishes. That response will come when the time is right. The key to good meditation is to focus completely on what you're doing. That doesn't mean tensing up and demanding. You need to be tranquil and open-minded. The more often you use your crystal in this way, the easier you will find it to relax into its vibrations.

As always, remember that your crystal will need cleansing and reprogramming at regular intervals.

Any crystal can be used as an aid to meditation, but the following are particularly helpful

Amethyst

This is the supreme meditation stone. Using it for meditation will guide you to the spiritual side of your nature. If you have difficulties with a session of meditation try placing an amethyst crystal over your Third Eye (the space between your eyebrows.)

Clear Quartz

This is an excellent crystal for meditation because it helps filter out any distractions. It harmonizes the mental energies that promote both awareness and peace of mind. If you use a single terminated quartz crystal, hold it with the point facing you to receive light and energy and answers to your questions. Holding it with the point facing away from you will project your thoughts to the universe.

Smoky Quartz

This is used to clarify your priorities and what you need to do to achieve spiritual awareness. Smoky quartz also helps to unite fragmented energies. If you are feeling at all depressed when you start your meditation, smoky quartz will lighten your spirits by the time the session ends.

Calcite

This helps you to dissociate yourself with the physical world and is a great aid to spiritual meditation.

Black Onyx

This assists with both grounding and relaxing the mind and enhances concentration.

Sodalite

This helps the transition from the mundane to the spiritual during your meditation.

Aragonite

This will calm and focus the mind, allowing the user to forget the outside world and relax into meditation.

Lapis Lazuli

This acts as a guide toward the higher planes of consciousness.

Malachite

This provides awareness of your own capabilities and limitations, bringing about a more harmonious situation in your life.

Rose Quartz

This establishes contact with the spirit world and brings tranquility. It enhances meditation by harmonizing and balancing variations in energy levels.

Black Tourmaline

This helps to maintain the meditative state and prevents the mind from wandering.

Although the crystals mentioned above are helpful, you should experiment with the other stones you possess, particularly those with which you feel a special affinity. As you become increasingly attuned to the process of meditation, you will know instinctively which crystals are best to use on any given day. As with all crystal work, this is largely a matter of personal intuition and belief.

Healing
with
Crystals

7

Crystals and gemstones have been used for centuries for healing spiritual, emotional, and physical problems. Today they are probably used more widely than ever before.

The crystals themselves do not do the healing. They act as conductors for the healing energy, which brings about recovery. Although any crystal will help with healing if it is programmed correctly, each type of crystal possesses its own energies. Crystals all vibrate at different frequencies. Hence some are more suitable than others for healing specific problems and will consequently be appropriate for dealing with certain aspects of the human condition.

Crystals formed as the globe was cooling, so they embody the life forces of the earth. It is this energy with which we bond. If you want the best and quickest results, consult the chart on page 76 to discover which crystal will be most useful for your personal needs.

Crystals may be used to treat various complaints in different parts of the body, neutralizing negative energies, and clearing blockages. However, they treat the body as a whole rather than merely alleviating the symptoms—which is the modern concept of holistic medicine.

When your crystal has been cleansed, programmed, and charged, keep it close to your body for as long as possible. The usual method is to wear the crystal in a pouch or as a pendant that is worn round the neck, keeping it near to the heart. It may also be carried in a pocket, but ideally it should be in contact with your body. If you prefer not to wear the crystal at night, place it under your pillow. The vibrations of the crystal will then steadily restore any imbalanced areas to a positive state.

The time taken to achieve results will vary according to many factors. These include the quality and size of the crystal, its energy charge, where and how long you wear it. Much also depends on selecting the crystal most appropriate to the problems you are experiencing.

Avoid wearing more than two crystals at any one time. This could result in a clash of energies, canceling the possible helpful effects from each stone.

Healing Properties of Specific Crystals

Agate

There are several types of agate and each has its own healing properties, but they can all be used to help produce serenity, both in the individual and in the environment.

Common agate is useful for helping to treat problems associated with the intestinal tract and the digestive system. It can also be used to alleviate the symptoms associated with emotional upsets.

Blue lace agate is the most effective agate for soothing the troubled mind, and for neutralizing fevers and general infections. This is a very calming stone and its effects can often be felt immediately, simply by holding the crystal in your hand. Try holding a piece of blue lace agate when you are angry and notice how your fury fades away.

Tree agate, with its beautiful branching inclusions, helps to heal the nervous system and the blood vascular system, both of which are structures that branch throughout the body.

Fire agate is used for helping those who have eye problems. This can range from difficulties focusing through conjunctivitis to glaucoma. However, it can also be used to aid clearer inner vision and insight.

Moss agate can be used as an aid to recovery, whatever the problem has been, regardless of whether it is mental or physical. It is especially efficacious for use after long-term illness and major surgery.

Amber

This material has been used for healing throat problems since at least Roman times. It is most effective for curing throat disorders but also for relieving respiratory problems and any related pain. Amber also helps to relieve depression.

Amethyst

This mainly works on the head—both physically and mentally. It is a useful crystal to keep handy if you suffer from headaches. Take a tumbled crystal and smooth it across the forehead whenever you feel a headache threatening. On the mental level, a small bed of amethyst points on the desk or bedside table is invaluable as an aid to stimulating the intuition.

Aquamarine

This is a useful stone to carry if you are subject to panic attacks. It has a strong calming effect and quickly soothes the nerves. It is also helpful in stressful conditions. Carry one when such situations are likely to occur and palm it until the nervous tension has eased.

Bloodstone

As its name suggests, this is the crystal to use as a remedy for diseases of the blood, especially where any poisoning is suspected. It also aids the circulation, detoxifies and cleanses the vascular system, heart, liver, kidneys, and spleen. Bloodstone is also a great energizer, and helps with overcoming feelings of inertia and apathy.

Carnelian

This helps with most problems of the abdomen and lower back—from the kidneys and lumbago to the reproductive organs of both sexes. It is also a great stimulator of the digestive process and aids the assimilation of both vitamins and minerals, consequently helping to restore flagging vitality. In addition, carnelian helps with rheumatism, neuralgia, arthritis, and depression.

Citrine

This stone helps to eliminate toxins from the body and fight infections, especially those that are exacerbated by poor circulation and where the immune system needs strengthening. It can also be used to help to boost the body's elimination process by stimulating the colon. It is particularly efficacious in helping to overcome phobias and alleviating unnecessary fears.

Clear Quartz

This is recognized as being the most potent of all the healing crystals. It is remarkably powerful but also gentle as its energy is discharged quite slowly. Clear quartz can be used for healing any form of sickness, even when the diagnosis is not clear. It has the unique ability to tune in to the person using it, rather than the user needing to attune to the crystal. For this reason, clear quartz is appropriate for healing both children and animals.

Coral

In all its varieties and colors, coral can be used in connection with any problem with the bones, including the teeth. It is particularly helpful in cases of osteoarthritis. Coral may also be used to help cure colic and other stomach disorders in the young.

Diamond

This is usually available only in small crystals, due to its rarity and cost. Nevertheless, even the smallest diamond has great potential for healing. Used alone, a diamond is useful as a healing crystal for eye problems, especially glaucoma. It also works well when used alongside other crystals as it enhances their power and properties. Diamond is one of the few crystals that never needs recharging.

Emerald

Although not a cure-all, it is capable of healing a number of complaints. An emerald will help to relieve eyestrain and is used to treat the heart, lungs, and nausea. It is also deals effectively with liver problems, most noticeably for detoxification. Emeralds should be in every crystal healing kit, but don't feel that you have to buy a cut and polished stone that would probably bankrupt you. The raw emerald, with all its imperfections and inclusions, is relatively inexpensive and for healing, it works just as well.

Garnet

This is found in many forms and many colors, and all are equally effective for use as healing crystals. A garnet will help to restore flagging energies through its ability to stimulate the metabolism. It will also encourage the digestive system to function more efficiently. It helps with lung problems, and acts as a revitalizing tonic on the heart and the vascular system.

Rose Quartz

This is the great emotional healing crystal. It will mend broken hearts, dispelling the negative vibrations caused when you are overwhelmed with grief. Its gentle vibrations also have a strengthening therapeutic effect on the physical heart. Rose quartz is unequalled in the treatment of headaches and migraines. Carrying or wearing this crystal will also help those who are struggling to overcome any type of addiction. Pass a polished tumbled rose quartz pebble over a bruise to ease the pain and help the injury to heal more quickly.

Ruby

This is a particularly powerful healing crystal for all conditions related to the vascular system and its associated organs, such as the heart and the liver. It is a potent detoxifier, aiding more effective blood circulation and helping to combat anemia. Rubies, like emeralds, are expensive but the raw uncut stone is perfectly adequate for use in healing.

Sapphire

This is an excellent stone for helping those who are stressed, frustrated and/or clinically depressed since it restores the mind's natural tranquility and equilibrium. For this reason it is useful to carry a sapphire with you if you are subject to panic attacks.

Smoky Quartz

This is an ideal crystal to have at your bedside if you suffer from insomnia. It has the ability to lower blood pressure and balance metabolism, thus aiding sleep. Smoky quartz will also dispel cramps and regulate the retention of liquid, particularly for those who suffer PMS. When buying this stone, ensure that it is absolutely natural and has not been artificially produced or colored. Use a reputable dealer and don't be afraid to ask questions.

Tiger's Eye

This is a useful crystal to have around if you have broken any bones as it assists with the healing process and the knitting together of fractures. In addition, tiger's eye heals throat problems and benefits the digestive system and the eyes.

Turquoise

This is a useful crystal for strengthening the immune system and as an aid to the regeneration of damaged tissues. It also provides an effective remedy for viral infections and a safeguard against environmental pollutants. When buying turquoise, do be careful to obtain the natural stone, as there are many fakes on the market.

Crystals and Chakra Healing

The chakras are seven centers of energy that can be found within the body of every human being. *Chakras* is a Sanskrit term meaning "wheels of light." Thus, in many books, the chakras are illustrated as vibrating wheels or—more romantically—as lotus flowers. Each chakra represents a power point, relating to a certain aspect of the human body.

Locations of the Chakras

1.   The Crown chakra—on the top (the crown) of the head.
2.   The Brow chakra—between the eyebrows (the third eye).
3.   The Throat chakra—under the Adam's apple.
4.   The Heart chakra—in the center of the chest.
5.   The Solar Plexus chakra—level with the navel.
6.   The Sacral chakra—level with the top of the pelvis.
7.   The Root chakra—level with the reproductive organs.

Finding Your Own Chakras

There is a simple method for finding the chakras within your own body. All you need to do is to close your eyes and hold the palms of your hands about an inch away from the locations (listed above) of the chakra you are seeking. Breathing regularly, visualize a soft white light glowing between your palms and your body. You will probably be surprised at how quickly you will feel energy streaming from the relevant chakra. However, don't be disheartened if your first attempt is unsuccessful. You may need to repeat the experiment several times. If you feel yourself becoming tense

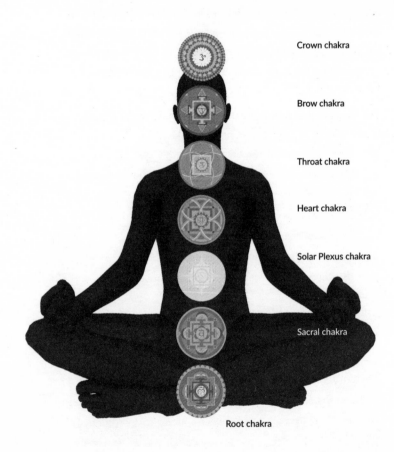

Crown chakra

Brow chakra

Throat chakra

Heart chakra

Solar Plexus chakra

Sacral chakra

Root chakra

and anxious, postpone your second attempt for a day or so. It is important to remain relaxed and calm.

All of these power points are highly susceptible to external energy forces, including crystals. Each chakra is associated with a specific color and, as you will see, this is the color of the crystal most frequently used in this form of healing.

Chakras and Crystal Colors

The colors of the chakras are the same as those of the rainbow.

Crown Chakra

Color—violet   Crystal—clear quartz or amethyst

Brow Chakra

Color—purple   Crystal—sodalite or lapis lazuli

Throat Chakra

Color—blue   Crystal—sapphire

Heart Chakra

Color—green   Crystal—emerald or agate

Solar Plexus Chakra

Color—yellow   Crystal—topaz or amber

Sacral Chakra

Color—orange   Crystal—tiger's eye or sunstone

Root Chakra

Color—red   Crystal—garnet

Chakras and Astrological Alignments

The Crown chakra is associated with the sign of Capricorn and the planet Saturn.

The Brow chakra is associated with the sign of Pisces and the planet Jupiter.

The Throat chakra is associated with the sign of Virgo and the planet Mercury.

The Heart chakra is associated with the sign of Libra and the planet Venus.

The Solar Plexus chakra is associated with the sign of Leo and with the Sun.

The Sacral chakra is associated with the sign of Cancer and the Moon.

The Root Chakra is associated with sign of Scorpio and the planet Mars.

Healing Through the Chakras

Combining crystals and the chakras for self-healing is very simple and it is absolutely safe. Such healing should take place in a quiet, pleasantly warm room with subdued lighting. If you wish to enhance the atmosphere, you may burn incense, light candles and/or have music playing quietly in the background. Try to ensure that you will not be interrupted during the session.

Now make yourself comfortable. It is immaterial whether you lie on a bed or on the floor, or relax in an armchair. Any position in which you feel most comfortable is the right one. Close your eyes for a few minutes, breathing regularly. Then begin to concentrate gently on the chakra associated with the problem you wish to heal.

Treatment Method

Activate the Crown chakra by using a clear quartz crystal for problems connected with the head, the glandular system, and depression.

Hold the crystal with the tip pointing down toward the head, a couple of inches above the crown. You will probably experience a tingling feeling or see flashing lights. This indicates that the crystal is activating the chakra. Holding your arms above your head may swiftly become uncomfortable but—if possible—maintain the position until the reactions fade. Regular repetition of this procedure will produce noticeable effects.

Activate the Brow chakra by using an amethyst or sodalite crystal for dealing with eye problems, blocked sinuses, earache, insomnia, and migraine.

Proceed as above, holding the crystal about two inches in front of your forehead with the point toward you. You will probably feel the energy flowing from the crystal into your forehead, possibly as a slight stabbing sensation. Again, maintain the position until these effects fade. Used regularly in this way, amethyst, or sodalite will also help to disperse fears and phobias.

Activate the Throat chakra by using a sapphire crystal for thyroid problems, sore throats, and stress.

This time, hold the crystal in front of the throat with the tip pointing toward the Adam's apple. When you feel warmth flowing from the crystal, you will know that the healing is working.

Activate the Heart chakra by using rose quartz for healing chest or heart problems, the breasts, arms, and circulation. This method also increases resistance to infection.

As always, direct the point of the crystal toward the relevant area—the center of the chest. The result will probably be a distinct tingling sensation. Don't be alarmed if you suddenly burst into tears. This indicates a release of repressed emotion.

Activate the Solar Plexus chakra by using a yellow crystal, such as amber or topaz, for digestive ailments. This chakra also affects the ego and will power.

Pointing one of these crystals toward the solar plexus will produce a steady throbbing sensation. When this subsides, the healing is complete.

Activate the Sacral chakra by using a tiger's eye or sunstone crystal to deal with kidney problems, fluid retention, and the menopause. This chakra also links with moodiness and emotional difficulties.

Hold the chosen crystal pointing toward the navel. The resulting warmth spreading throughout the body will produce relaxation and serenity, as well as enhancing your "get-up-and-go."

Activate the Root chakra by using a garnet or obsidian crystal for healing sexual problems, constipation, or irritable bowel syndrome. Irritability, fear, and anger also respond to this chakra.

Point the crystal toward the base of the abdomen and you should swiftly feel warmth and a release of tension throughout the area.

The system described above is simple to use and extremely effective. However, some practitioners believe that even better results are produced if the patient is lying down and the crystal is placed on the appropriate chakra in contact with the skin, rather than on top of the clothing. The technique for both systems is simple, and the results are usually powerful. Use whichever method most appeals to you and suits your circumstances.

Note: *It is essential to cleanse and reprogram your crystal after every healing session.*

Crystals for Comment Ailments

Here is a list of crystals that you can use to help the body to overcome common ailments.

IMPORTANT NOTE

The crystals mentioned here are not recommended as an alternative to professional medical attention. It is important that if you feel unwell, you should consult a qualified physician. The crystals we list may aid the healing process and/or alleviate symptoms, but must on no account be used until accurate medical diagnosis and appropriate treatment has been given.

AILMENT	CRYSTAL
Abdominal pains	White coral
Aggression	Bloodstone
Alcoholism	Amethyst
Anemia	Bloodstone, citrine, ruby
Arthritis	Azurite, garnet, malachite
Asthma	Amber, jade
Back problems	Hematite, sapphire
Biliousness	Emerald, jade
Bladder problems	Jade, jasper, tourmaline
Blood pressure (high)	Chrysoprase, emerald
Blood pressure (low)	Ruby, tourmaline
Boils	Agate, sapphire
Bones (aching)	Rose quartz, spinel

AILMENT	CRYSTAL
Bowel problems	Yellow jasper
Brain tonic	Coral, lapis lazuli
Breathlessness	Amber, jet
Bronchitis	Amber, jet
Bruises	Rose quartz
Burns	Chrysoprase, jadeite
Catarrh	Amber, topaz
Central Nervous System	Aventurine
Chest pains	Amber, emerald, dioptase
Chicken Pox	Pearl, topaz
Circulatory problems	Blue John, ruby
Colic	Coral, jade, malachite
Common cold	Emerald, jet
Constipation	Emerald, ruby
Convulsions	Coral, zircon
Coughs	Amber, topaz
Cramp	Bloodstone, flint
Depression	Jade, lapis lazuli, rhodocrosite
Diabetes	Diamond, bloodstone, jasper
Diarrhea	Malachite
Dizziness	Sapphire
Dysentery	Emerald
Earache	Amber, sapphire, tourmaline
Eczema	Sapphire

AILMENT	CRYSTAL
Eye strain	Emerald, opal, topaz
Fainting spells	Lapis lazuli
Fatigue	Hematite, rose quartz
Fever	Amber, moonstone
Flatulence	Emerald, green garnet
Gallstones	Bloodstone, rock crystal
Gastric ulcers	Emerald, sapphire
Hemorrhage (minor)	Ruby
Hemorrhoids	Bloodstone, topaz
Hay Fever	Amber, jet, zircon
Headache	Amethyst, hematite
Heartburn	Emerald, olivine
Indigestion	Olivine
Insomnia	Amethyst, sodalite
Kidney problems	Bloodstone, jade, malachite
Liver complaints	Emerald, jade, ruby
Lumbago	Magnetite, sapphire
Measles, Rubella	Pearl, topaz
Menopause	Garnet, lapis lazuli, pearl
Mumps	Topaz
Nephritis	Jade
Nervousness	Jade, sapphire
Neuralgia	Amethyst, lapis lazuli
Nightmares	Hematite, jet, ruby

AILMENT	CRYSTAL
Nose bleeds	Ruby, sapphire
Pancreatic problems	Diamond, bloodstone, jasper
Premenstrual Stress (PMS)	Smoky quartz,
Quinsy	Amber, jet, topaz
Rheumatism	Azurite, malachite
Sciatica	Sapphire, tourmaline
Shingles	Jadeite, lapis lazuli
Sinus problems	Jet
Stomach ailments	Amethyst, coral, jade
Stomach pains	Aquamarine, lapis lazuli
Stomach ulcers	Sapphire
Stress	Citrine, rose quartz, turquoise
Swollen glands	Topaz
Throat complaints	Amber, hematite, tourmaline
Thyroid problems	Lapis lazuli, rhodonite
Tonsillitis	Amber, tourmaline
Toothache	Amber, jet
Urinary disorders	Amber, jade
Varicose veins	Amber, aquamarine, opal
Wounds, to aid healing	Garnet, hematite, ruby

A Gallery
of Crystals

8

Agates

Agate (often called the Fire stone) is traditionally considered to have protective powers and is sometimes referred to as "a gate" to a better spiritual outlook, courage and fortitude. Sources include America, Brazil, and India.

It is found in many forms and a multitude of colors. Large crystals are often cut into slices to display the colorful bands within the stone.

Blue lace agate is one of the most popular forms of this crystal. It is pale blue, banded with white or darker lines, usually available as a small tumbled stone.

Moss agate is particularly interesting. This is a transparent crystal containing what appear to be streaks of green moss. Depending on the color of these inclusions, moss agate is also known as the Mocha stone or the Tree agate. Yet another name, this time for a yellowish green variety, is amberine.

Sylvester stones contain two colored bands, one light and one dark. Owl's eye is the name given to a crystal bearing two sets of black circles. Blood agate is another name for the red agate. The fire agate is especially beautiful, its depth of glowing color being created by iron oxide deposits.

All types and colors of agate are readily obtainable. It is well to remember, though, that the brilliant colors are not always natural to the stone, having been produced by dyeing or staining. These can be very attractive but, if the natural stone is what you are after, be sure to ask before you buy.

Agates have a balancing, grounding effect, providing emotional and physical security, particularly when traveling. They can relieve stress and help to establish a peaceful atmosphere.

Physically, they are known to protect the pancreas, circulatory, immune and lymphatic systems and to support the colon.

Amber

Strictly speaking, amber is not a crystal, but like coral and jet, it is popularly regarded as a gemstone and therefore merits inclusion in this book.

Amber is actually fossilized resin that dripped from certain trees millions of years ago. It often contains insects or fragments of foliage that were trapped while the resin was still liquid. Thus, anyone wearing a piece of amber can claim a link to times before the Ice Age—a romantic and mysterious idea.

This stone is usually a beautiful golden color. It may be opaque or transparent, but always gleams like solidified sunshine. Amber also comes in shades of purple, red, brown, and black, but the most valuable stones are blue or green and are much sought after by collectors.

The color of the stone often depends upon the area in which it was found. Burmese amber (sometimes known as burmite) is often red or brown, while Rumanian amber (rumanite) is such a dark red that it seems almost black. Another type of amber appears cloudy due to the number of air bubbles it contains.

This is often pale yellow with a milky appearance. In the 1920s, this type of amber (known as bastard amber) was often used for bead necklaces for the "flappers" of the period, but is now seldom seen.

Amber jewelry, often set in silver, is currently extremely popular and is usually reasonably priced. However, it is well to remember that you get what you pay for. In other words, examine your purchases carefully to ensure that they are unflawed and that they are, indeed, amber. Some plastic beads can look remarkably convincing.

Even today, the medical uses of amber continue in a variety of ways. Oil of amber is used in the preparation of liniments, and it is said that water in which amber has been steeped provides a gentle laxative. The application of the stones themselves is also recommended for a number of conditions such as memory loss, breathing problems, and lack of energy. Wearing amber is claimed to promote a feeling of general well being.

Amethyst

Sometimes known as "the elevator." This is a form of quartz, which comes in varying shades of purple, ranging from pale mauve to deepest violet. It is found in a number of countries worldwide, including Britain, Mexico, Russia, America, Sri Lanka, and India.

Large single amethysts are extremely rare—and therefore valuable. Smaller stones are often found in clusters (known as beds) forming what appears to be a cushion of sparkling purple. Most rock shops also have on display at least one amethyst druse—an arch of rock lined with the crystals. These are extremely beautiful—and expensive.

Amethyst is a popular crystal and is available in a variety of shapes and sizes, most commonly as jewelry. Prices vary widely according to the size and purity of the stones.

Amethyst has a gentle, calming effect and for this reason is highly valued as a healing stone. It is said to promote restful sleep when placed beneath the pillow, and it helps to ease headaches.

It strengthens the endocrine and immune systems and is thought to influence the pituitary glands. There is also a belief that amethyst is helpful for clairvoyance.

Aquamarine

The "Sea Stone" is a beautiful transparent crystal, either sea blue or sea green in color. The crystal's name is derived from the Latin *aqua marina*, which refers to its resemblance to deep clear seawater. The aquamarine is a beryl, which means that it comes from the same family as the emerald. It is equally beautiful though less valuable. Sources include Ireland, Mexico, Zimbabwe, and Afghanistan.

This stone is comparatively inexpensive and readily available from all rock shops and jewelers. When used as jewelry it is usually set in silver.

Aquamarine has long been regarded as possessing balancing qualities, endowing the wearer with a serene attitude. It is said to enhance clairvoyance and is widely used for meditation.

Aventurine

"The gambler's stone" is usually green, but comes also in brown, red, or yellow. It is an opaque stone, speckled with scales of mica. Sources include Brazil, China, Italy, India, and Russia.

Aventurine found in Delaware County, is known as delawarite. The green variety is sometimes called Indian Jade or the Stone of Heaven.

Aventurine (sometimes known as adventurine) is readily available and is often used for jewelry or for small, carved ornaments.

This is said to be the luckiest stone of all for gamblers, and poker players often use the red variety to attract good fortune. Aventurine has excellent balancing powers and can help with psychosomatic illnesses. Physically, this crystal is efficacious for skin troubles, alleviates urinary problems, and has a calming effect on nervous or hysterical people. Believed to increase visionary powers, it was used for the eyes of Tibetan statues.

Beryl

This is in fact a generic term for a variety of stones, all of which have been valued for thousands of years. Also known as *ponzoon* (meaning "all life"), it is particularly associated with love and with psychic work of all kinds. Sources include Russia, Australia, Norway, and Brazil.

Beryl comes in several colors, each bearing its own name. A greenish-yellow stone is known as aquamarine chrysolite. The bright green type is better known as emerald. Aquamarine is the name for sea blue and sea green beryls. Morganite is pink, and the yellow type is known as heliodor, which means "gift from the sun."

All types of beryl are easily obtainable but prices tend to reflect the rarity of the stone.

Each type of beryl possesses a specific power of its own, but the crystals in general are known to be particularly helpful in developing psychic abilities. St. Hildegard regarded beryl as an antidote for poison, and early Christians knew it as St. Thomas' Stone.

Bloodstone (also known as heliotrope or St. Stephen's stone) is composed of dark green quartz spotted with red or yellow jasper. It is found in Australia, Brazil, China, and Russia.

This stone is easily obtainable from rock shops, though it is rarely used in making jewelry, and usually comes as a large, polished pebble.

In ancient times, bloodstone was thought to possess incredible magical properties—controlling the weather, for example. Today it is still regarded as a powerful stone, increasing creativity and courage. It is also claimed to reduce impatience and irritability.

Calcite

This is a very common crystal and we know that it was used as far back as 1000 BC. It is found all over the world and sources include America, Britain, Slovakia, Peru, Iceland, and Brazil.

Calcite can be blue, green, orange, yellow, pink, red or colorless. The good quality colorless variety is known as Iceland spar and is considered to help the vision. Calcite is translucent and sometimes banded. Names for the banded version include Egyptian alabaster and Mexican onyx. If the stone has been dyed green it is sometimes known as Mexican jade. Other names for calcite include silverstone and Oriental alabaster.

All types and colors of calcite are readily available. However, it is not unusual for this stone to be acid-treated in order to enhance the color.

Blue calcite is reputed to be helpful for problems with the lungs and the voice. The orange version can help with digestive problems. Green calcite was considered by the Native Americans to represent the small woodland spirits. The stones were used in ceremonies to welcome visitors in the belief that the spirits would ensure that the donors would be liberally repaid.

Carnelian

This stone is sometimes called "the Friendly One." This is usually a rich, deep brownish red and is said to be named after the kornel cherry, which is the same color. A 17th century physician, Johann Schroeder, had a different opinion, describing it as half transparent and like bloody flesh! However, it can also be found in other colors, such as blue, green, and even white. Carnelians are found in Czechoslovakia, Peru, Britain, Iceland, and Romania.

The carnelian is a common crystal, widely available, and inexpensive. A carved carnelian was often used in a signet ring, where the intaglio could be used as a seal.

Carnelian is much prized as a healing stone and is said to enhance concentration. It is also claimed to alleviate shyness, help with spinal problems, and protect against dysfunction of the liver, lungs, and pancreas.

Celestite/Celestine

These are two names used for the same crystal. It is also called the "Stone of Heaven" because people once thought it had been created by the music of the celestial choirs. This is a transparent crystal, usually found in large pieces or as a geode. It is found in Britain, Mexico, Peru, Poland, and Madagascar.

This stone comes in yellow, orange, red, and white—these varieties may be known as celestite. *Celestine* is the usual name for the blue variety of this crystal.

Another variety, which geologists tell us has been compressed in the ground for millions of years, is known as *angelite*. This is considered an extremely powerful crystal.

These stones are very brittle and likely to crumble. All types of these crystals are easily obtainable but are likely to be expensive because of their fragility.

These stones are considered to be particularly helpful for people in the performing arts and are said to cure stage fright. Angelite is thought to harmonize all aspects of the person—mind, body, and spirit—and to bring peace to difficult situations.

Celestine is general classed as a "New Age" stone and is thought to encourage enlightenment. It is a particularly creative stone.

Chalcedony

This is usually a transparent stone, sometimes banded. It is available in a variety of sizes, ranging from small tumbled stones to geodes. Sources include Austria, Slovakia, Iceland, Britain, and other countries worldwide.

Chalcedony is found in a number of colors and under several names. The white variety is known as milkstone. Blue chalcedony is known as the blue moonstone, and the lilac color is called Mojave moonstone. Opaline is the name given to the opalescent yellow type.

This crystal is readily obtainable at reasonable prices.

The Greeks used this crystal as an amulet to protect sailors against drowning. It is believed to increase good humor and prevent irritability. In the Middle Ages it was used to treat insanity, and it symbolized chastity. Today it is thought to be helpful in dealing with panic attacks.

Citrine

This is a lovely yellow or brown stone, very similar to the topaz. Indeed, it is variously known as the Brazilian topaz, false topaz, and Scotch topaz. It also exists in a smoky gray version. This stone is found in Britain and America, Russia, Madagascar, and Brazil.

Natural citrine is comparatively rare, though it is available in rock shops and from jewelers. Check carefully when you buy this crystal since heat-treated amethyst is sometimes passed off as citrine.

Citrine is considered extremely helpful for healing and self-development and is even said to increase wealth. This is one of the few crystals that never need to be cleansed, and is thought to be highly protective,

Clear Quartz

This is also known as rock crystal, commonly called "the all singing, all dancing stone"; it is the most popular of all the crystals. As its name suggests, clear quartz is transparent—almost like glass—and can be identified by its six-sided crystalline form. It is often cloudy or milky at one end, where it was attached to the earth, its transparency increasing toward the peak of the crystal.

True clear quartz is colorless but in certain lights, it may sometimes appear to contain "rainbows." Colored varieties of quartz are defined under separate names—see amethyst, citrine, rose quartz, smoky quartz.

Rutilated quartz is much sought after and is perhaps the loveliest of all the quartz crystals. It is totally transparent and contains long fine golden crystals resembling hairs. Hence its popular name—the Venus hair stone.

Herkimer diamonds are another type of clear quartz, remarkable for their clarity and sparkle. Most crystals develop in the earth, but "Herkies" are formed in water, and are found only in Herkimer County, NY.

Quartz comes in many shapes: in clusters, chunks, and wands or in smooth, machine-polished pebbles. These come in many sizes, from tiny sparkling fragments found on beaches to an enormous single crystal once found in India. It was six feet tall and measured three feet across.

Clear quartz is inexpensive and readily obtainable. Indeed, beaches throughout the world are comprised of minute quartz crystals and many granite buildings appear to sparkle in the sun because of the quartz embedded in the stone. However, there is no need to sweep a beach or deface a granite building to obtain a piece of clear quartz for your own use since the crystal is available in all rock stores.

Quartz is regarded as something of a cure-all and is said to adjust its energy to the needs of the person using the crystal. Both physically and mentally, it is regarded as a powerful healing stone.

Coral

This is an organic gemstone. It is not a mineral and therefore, strictly speaking, it is not a crystal. It is formed from the minute skeletons of coral polyps that gradually build up to form massive reefs in the sea.

It comes in a variety of colors, the most popular of which is red, known as arciscuro, rosso scuro, and rosso, depending on the depth of the color. Other colors include pink, ranging from salmon to pale rose, and a particularly lovely shade—*pelle d'angello*. This is sometimes referred to as "angel skin" and is much sought after by collectors. More rarely, coral is available in blue, black and an attractive golden color, found off the coast of Japan.

Coral has always been associated with children, and at one time, every small girl's first item of jewelry was a coral necklace. Childhood photographs of Queen Elizabeth II show her wearing one. A 16th century writer advised that it was "good to be hanged around the neck of children" and claimed that if the wearer was ill, the coral would "turn pale and wan."

Coral has always been regarded as a protective stone and was particularly popular with sailors. It was believed, too, to protect children from "the falling sickness," teething problems, and to frighten away evil spirits.

Diamond

This is the hardest crystal known to man. It is so hard that only specialist diamond cutters who employ a number of complex techniques can produce the beautiful stones that are used so widely in jewelry. Because of its hardness, the Greeks called it *adamas*, meaning "hard" or "untamable." This is the origin of the term "adamantine" used to describe the diamond's unique luster. The stones are mined in Africa, Brazil, Australia, India, and America.

Popularly known as "King of the Stones," diamonds come in a variety of colors in addition to the most popular, colorless version. Naturally available in yellow, pink, green, blue, brown, and even black—they can be irradiated to produce blue, gold, purple, green, red, or yellow shades.

Diamonds have always been regarded as protective stones and, for this reason, were thought to be hated by the devil. They are also said to attract wealth and to increase energy.

Like quartz, diamonds are currently used in a variety of industrial and commercial ways. Diamonds are readily available but extremely expensive.

Emerald

This is a brilliant green crystal, known as "the Stone of Spring," and was once thought to bestow eternal youth. These stones are found in India, Zimbabwe, Austria, Brazil, Egypt, and Tanzania.

Raw, unpolished emeralds are readily available in rock shops, but the cut, polished gems used for jewelry are extremely expensive.

Emeralds are said to increase inspiration and to endow the wearer with patience. They are believed to enhance the memory and endow the wearer with the ability to see situations clearly. The stones have always been associated with fertility and birth and also with the eyes. The Emperor Nero is said to have had an emerald eyeglass, but this is unlikely as the stones are usually much too clouded for this purpose.

Fluorite

In its clear version, fluorite can sometimes be mistaken for a diamond. Like celestine, this is regarded as a "New Age" stone.

Sources include Australia, America, Britain, Germany, China, and Mexico.

Fluorite comes in blue, green, purple, yellow, and brown in addition to the clear variety mentioned above. Blue John is a type of fluorite and the green version is sometimes known as the African Emerald. It is also known as fluorspar.

This crystal is widely available and inexpensive.

Almost nothing is known about the historical uses of fluorite but today it is believed that the clear variety will clarify thinking and produce positive action. It is thought to strengthen the teeth and bones and to be extremely protective, particularly on the psychic level. Fluorite is also considered to be very effective as a protection against negative vibrations from computers and other similar machines.

Garnet

The "garnet" originates from the Latin word *grenat*, which means pomegranate. This was probably because small garnets are similar in appearance to pomegranate seeds. These crystals are found all over the world.

Though it is generally supposed to be red, garnet comes in a rainbow of colors—colorless to deep red, violet, orange, green, yellow, purple, brown, and black. Despite this wide variety of shades, a blue garnet has never been discovered.

This is a common stone and readily available from rock shops or jewelers.

Garnet is believed to alleviate any problems with the blood and circulation and is regarded as an excellent energizing stone. At one time it was regarded as a talisman, in view of its protective properties. It is also regarded as a stimulant, particularly useful in sorting out complex situations. A square cut garnet is thought to resolve business problems and bring about success.

Hematite

This is a dark stone, containing iron, and said to be extremely powerful. It is found in Italy, Britain, Sweden, Canada, and Switzerland.

Hematite is usually black or gray, though there is a red variety. It comes in a wide variety of sizes and is usually polished. There is also a brown variety, known as limonite. Other names for hematite include Alaska black diamond, Dutch bloodstone, and volcano spit (presumably a reference to its iron content.)

This crystal is readily obtainable and inexpensive. It is often used to make extremely attractive jewelry.

This crystal is considered to provide stability and to ensure a good outcome in legal matters—hence its popular name as the Lawyers' Stone—being particularly effective for healing community disputes. It is a good grounding stone and increases personal charisma. In Voodoo it is used for good luck in gambling, to influence lovers and to protect against illness.

Jade

This is generally considered to be a green stone, though it is also found as orange, brown, blue, blue-green, lavender, red—and even cream or white. It is usually considered to be a Chinese crystal but is also found in America, Italy, Russia, and the Middle East.

It is not widely known that, in fact, two separate stones are commonly known as jade. One is jadeite, the other nephrite. In China, jade was commonly known as "the Emperor's Stone." The green varieties were extremely valuable and are known as Imperial Jade. Nephrite has a number of names—axe stone, kidney stone, New Zealand greenstone, and Wyoming jade. White nephrite is sometimes called mutton fat jade and the deep green type found in Siberia is also called spinach green jade. Bowenite is the name given to a crystal called "new jade," said to be much more powerful than jade itself.

Jade is invariably expensive, and some colors are extremely rare. Nephrite is more easily obtainable than jadeite.

Innumerable attributes are allocated to jade, depending on the country of origin. It has always been regarded as a valuable and magical crystal. If you are interested, you will find a study of its history absolutely fascinating.

Jasper

This is available in a variety of colors and shades, each of which has its own specific qualities. It is a common crystal, found throughout the world.

Other names for this stone include iaspere, iaspar, jasp, jaspre, and silex. Leek-green jasper is known both as plasma and mother-of-emerald, while the type obtained from Vancouver Island is called dallasite. Black jasper is known as touchstone and lapis lydius, while striped versions of the crystal are called ribbon jasper.

It is readily available at reasonable prices in all rock shops.

Much used for amulets, jasper was thought to bestow immunity from possession by evil spirits and from insanity. Green jasper, much used by traders, was said to bring good luck in business. Native Americans called the crystal "the Rain Bringer," a belief shared with the Greeks. St. Hildegard suggested that holding a piece of jasper in the hand during childbirth would protect both mother and child from the demons of the air. In Elizabethan England, green jasper was widely used for healing by physicians who called it "the spleen stone."

Jet

Like amber, the use of jet is extremely ancient. It was used during the Bronze Age. It has been discovered in prehistoric graves and in countries all over the world and is believed to be one of the first crystals used by man.

There is only one variety of jet and it comes in only one color—coal black. It has many names, including black amber, witches amber, gate, gette, ieate, and jesstone. Whitby jet carved into the shape of a cross is particularly popular in Yorkshire, England.

Mined in just about every country in the world, jet is readily available from jewelers and rock shops.

Jet has always been used to make jewelry but became particularly popular in Victorian England, when the Queen wore it after the death of the Prince Consort. It is said that jet should always be set in silver. Legend has it that jet became part of the wearer's body—a slightly macabre idea if buying it secondhand. In any case, care should be taken when purchasing that you are getting the genuine article; much of what is known as French jet is actually polished black glass.

Labradorite

This is a most unusual stone, little known until comparatively recently in the 18th century. Sources of supply include Italy, Greenland, Finland, and Scandinavia.

Labradorite comes in several colors, gray to black, sometimes white, all carrying "rainbows" when the stone catches the light. White labradorite is called rainbow moonstone, and the transparent variety is known as black moonstone (although this crystal is not, in fact, moonstone). It is also known as Labrador spar. A particularly iridescent type found in Finland is known as spectrolite. The yellow type is transparent.

All types of labradorite are readily available, usually as small polished pebbles.

This stone is often described as the rainbow bridge between the conscious and unconscious mind. In some northern countries it is thought to have dropped to earth from the aurora borealis. Labradorite strengthens the immune system and encourages beneficial change. It is also an inspirational stone, much used by novelists and composers.

Lapis Lazuli

Lapis lazuli is yet another stone that is sometimes called the "Stone of Heaven." It is found in Russia, Chile, Italy, America, Egypt, and the Middle East.

Lapis Lazuli is always deep blue, often flecked with gold pyrites. It has many names, including lazurite, the azure gem, the Armenian stone, and lapis lazari. It is thought that, when the Ancient Greeks mentioned "sapphire sprinkled with gold dust," they were actually referring to lapis lazuli.

This stone is expensive, but easily obtained at rock shops and from jewelers.

Ra, the Egyptian sun god, was said to have lapis lazuli hair. The Ancient Egyptians regarded lapis lazuli as being equal to gold in value. It is said that the first eye-shadow was made from this crushed crystal, probably because it is considered to aid vision. When crushed and mixed with milk and sediment from the River Nile, it was also believed to cure cataracts.

Malachite

This was known and used in Egypt as far back as 4000 BC. It is found in Romania, Zambia, Russia, and the Middle East. It is the ore from which copper is made.

Malachite is always green, but may vary in shade from light to very dark. It is often banded and these stones, when polished, are particularly beautiful. Some malachite is called "the Peacock Stone," because the patterns it contains resemble the tail of a peacock. It is also known as "the Sleep Stone," in the belief that staring at it for any length of time would induce slumber. It is associated with the planet, Venus.

This stone is used in a variety of ways, from small polished pebbles to bowls and platters. It is readily available, but the price increases in line with the way in which it is used.

Malachite is regarded as a "goddess stone," dedicated to Our Lady of the Mountains in Russia and to Freya in Viking countries. It is considered to be a highly protective stone with a variety of uses. These include curing colic and heart pains, helping teething babies, and protecting the owner from seduction. The peacock stone was prized in Italy as a protection against the evil eye, particularly if set in silver.

Moonstone

This is often regarded as "the Stone of New Beginnings" and as the name suggests, it is closely aligned with the waxing and waning of the moon. Sources include Australia, Sri Lanka, and India.

Moonstone comes in translucent shades of white, cream, yellow, blue and green. It is often known as "the Travelers' Stone" and, in the Middle Ages, was called selenite. These crystals are particularly abundant in Sri Lanka, where they are known as the Ceylon opal.

This crystal is mainly used for creating exquisite pieces of jewelry. Although it is readily obtainable, prices vary according to the quality of the setting.

This crystal is sacred to moon goddesses all over the world, including Aphrodite, the Greek goddess of love and Selene, her Roman counterpart. At one time it was believed that the color of the moonstone varied with the cycles of the moon. The stone is considered particularly valuable to women, helping with fertility, menstruation, pregnancy, and childbirth.

Obsidian

Obsidian is actually volcanic lava that cooled too quickly for it to crystallize. It comes mainly from Mexico but is also found in other volcanic areas.

Obsidian comes in a number of colors and several types. These include snowflake obsidian, a gray stone with flecks of white, and rainbow obsidian, a dark stone carrying bands of rainbow colors.

Apache Tears are small, transparent pebbles of dark obsidian. Other colors include black, brown, blue, green, and gray or silver.

The black/brown/gray stones are easy to come by, but some of the other colors are rare. Note that so-called blue-green obsidian is often man-made glass.

This crystal is considered a balancing and healing stone. According to the Aztecs, it was the source of life; they used it to heal wounds. The Mayans made "magic mirrors" of polished obsidian and John Dee, the Elizabethan Astrologer Royal, was also believed to use one for scrying.

Legend has it that the name "Apache Tears" originated in Arizona where a group of warriors were attacked and killed. It is said that the women of the tribe wept at the foot of the cliff and their tears became embedded in the obsidian pebbles.

Onyx

This has been popular for thousands of years and is considered to be particularly supportive in times of need. It is found in Mexico, America, Brazil, South Africa, and Italy.

Onyx can be black, gray, brown, white, blue, yellow, or red and has a marbled appearance. A number of names serve to distinguish between the colors. Red onyx is also known as sardonyx, while the white or gray-banded stone is called chalcedonyx. The term lynx-eye onyx is used for an onyx marked with a white circle. A layered form, comprising a thin blue-white layer over a thick black layer, is known as nicolo.

All types of this stone are easily available at affordable prices. Some years ago, onyx coffee tables were the height of fashion, as were lamp stands and other items of furniture. These are still available but are no longer as popular as they used to be.

All types of onyx are considered to be excellent as earthing and healing stones. It is considered to be particularly appropriate in times of stress and is said to aid in overcoming apathy. Sardonyx was thought to symbolize the honesty and sincerity of the Apostles James and Philip. In the 10th century, an onyx, too large to be held in one hand, was owned by the Abbey of St. Albans (England). This stone was thought to aid in childbirth. St. Hildegard recommended the use of onyx for eye problems. She instructed that the stone should be steeped for 30 days in pure wine. At the end of this period, the stone was removed and the eyes were bathed in the wine every night.

Opal

This is one of the most beautiful stones known to man and it is difficult to understand why it once had a reputation for being unlucky. The stones are mined in a number of countries throughout the world, including Australia, Mexico, Britain, Canada, and America.

Opal is available in a wide variety of colors, the colors often in the same stone. Some opals are clear or milky, others are iridescent, but very few lack the positive rainbow of colors typical of this crystal. The fire opal is particularly striking, as it contains a blaze of orange-red, but even the black opal appears to flash with color in certain lights.

These crystals are readily available, though the finer specimens may be expensive. They are mainly used in the production of jewelry.

The idea that opals brought bad luck changed during Victorian times, when the Queen began to give opal jewelry as wedding presents. Since then, this has been considered a lucky stone, said to strengthen the will to live, and to encourage persistence and stick-to-itiveness. Exhaustion and fatigue are thought to respond to its fiery power and it is said to bring good fortune to new businesses.

On a personal note, I believe there must be some kind of antipathy between opals and me, because every piece of opal jewelry that I have owned has immediately been stolen, gone missing, or crumbled into powder.

Peridot

This is a greenish stone, which was at one time mistakenly referred to as emerald. Sources include Brazil, America, Ireland, Russia, Sri Lanka, and the Canary Islands. Peridot is opaque, but becomes clear when polished and faceted.

It comes in varying shades of green, ranging from olive to brown.

This crystal is easily obtainable but really good stones are rare.

In the past, peridot was widely used for making talismans as it was said to repel evil spirits. Today it is regarded as a luck-bringer *par excellence*, ensuring wealth, love, and good fortune throughout life. In Ancient Egypt, the priests wore this stone to ensure they did not fall into jealousy and resentment.

Rose Quartz

This is popularly known as the love stone, though it is also called the American ruby and the Mont Blanc ruby. It is mined in South Africa, Brazil, Japan, Madagascar, and America.

Rock shops usually sell this as a tumbled stone, though larger pieces are available rough and unpolished. Whichever form it takes, this crystal comes in a beautiful shade of soft pink—though some are so pale as to be almost white.

This crystal is easily obtained from rock shops, often as jewelry.

Rose quartz is believed to enhance the wearer's appreciation of beauty. It is a very positive stone and is thought to help in overcoming negative thoughts and attitudes. This crystal is still believed to possess soothing qualities, but it was once thought to be so powerful that aggressive people could not survive in its presence.

This is the stone of unconditional love and peace.

Ruby

Ruby has always been considered to be one of the most powerful crystals for protection and healing. Mined in Russia, Madagascar, Cambodia, Kenya, and Mexico, it comes in all shades of red, some so dark as to be almost black. When polished, it is sparkling and transparent, but raw stones remain opaque.

Rubies in their natural state are widely available in rock shops. When the stones are polished and used in jewelry they are expensive.

This stone is thought to strengthen the immune system and is particularly effective for dealing with disorders of the blood. It is said to dispel negative attitudes, to increase concentration, and sharpen the mind.

Sapphire

Sapphire is usually known as a blue stone though it does, in fact, come in a variety of other colors including black, yellow, brown, orange, pink, green, purple, and colorless varieties. The name originates from the Greek *sappheiros*. These crystals are found in Brazil, India, Kenya, Australia, and Sri Lanka.

Cornflower blue is the most sought after color, though most of the blue sapphires on sale today are much darker. Star sapphires are particularly beautiful and are claimed to bring good fortune to their owner.

Most types of sapphire are easily obtainable, particularly as rough stones but some colors are quite rare. Star sapphires are much sought after.

This stone is said to enhance willpower and self-discipline and is helpful in solving mental problems. Each color of sapphire is thought to possess its own distinctive qualities—for example, the black sapphire is said to help in obtaining work and the yellow version is believed to bring wealth.

Selenite

Like all crystals, selenite has been around for thousands of years, but it is commonly regarded as a "New Age" stone. It is found in America, Mexico, Russia, Greece, Poland, England, and France.

Selenite is a ribbed translucent stone, usually white, but also available in orange-brown, blue, and green. The finely ribbed version is known as satin spar. There is also a type resembling a fish tail (sometimes called angel's wing) and another brownish variety called desert rose. Unlike most crystals, selenite sometimes grows naturally in the form of a wand. Tipped with other crystals, these are much prized.

Selenite is easily obtainable. It is usually reasonably priced, but wands can be very expensive.

This stone is said to protect the wearer against epilepsy and to improve the skin. It is regarded as a fertility stone, protecting pregnant woman as well as the child. Selenite enhances the stability of partnerships and encourages all types of communication.

Smoky Quartz

This is an attractive transparent stone, combining shades of amber, brown, and black. It comes in long, translucent crystals having darker points. This variety of quartz is found worldwide.

One extremely dark type of smoky quartz is known as radium diamond or morion. There is also a particularly brilliant form found in France known as the Alencon diamond.

It is readily available in rock shops but be careful that you are not fobbed off with an irradiated specimen. These are easily identifiable, as they are very dark and not transparent.

Smoky quartz is energizing and protective, often used to assist concentration. It is helpful in overcoming depression and is an efficient grounding stone.

Tiger's Eye

This stone is usually yellow or amber-brown, with a striped appearance, a pattern which in fact resembles the eye of a cat. Other colors such as blue, gold, and red colors are also available. Sources include South Africa, Mexico, India, Australia, and America.

This crystal was at one time known as *oculus celi* or crocidolite. There is also a type known as hawk's eye.

The most usual version of tiger's eye is the amber-brown one but other colors are quite readily obtainable, often as small tumbled stones.

This is an excellent energizing and protective stone, effective as a good luck charm or an amulet. It also possesses many healing qualities.

Topaz

Topaz been used in healing and divination for thousands of years. Usually found in transparent, pointed crystals, it is mined in Pakistan, Sri Lanka, Australia, America, and South Africa.

Although most people think of a topaz as being golden yellow, it actually comes in several other colors—orange, green, blue, pink, and colorless. The pink variety, which is rare, is often produced by heat treatment. The golden version is known as the Imperial Topaz.

You may need to go to a specialist store for a piece of raw topaz, although it is readily available in the form of jewelry. Prices vary, depending on the size, color, and quality of the stone.

Topaz is said to be beneficial for sight problems and may help in overcoming addictions. It reduces stress, gives strength, and will guard the home and the people in it. Imperial topaz will enhance your self-confidence and enable you to overcome any hindrances to your plans.

Turquoise

Sometimes referred to as "the Horseman's Stone" because it provides protection from falls, this is thought to be one of the first crystals used by man. This is an opaque stone, often polished, and comes in shades of turquoise, blue, or green. It is found in many locations, including China, Egypt, Mexico, Peru, Poland, Russia, Tibet, Afghanistan, and America.

Tibetan turquoise is green and is said to carry different vibrations from the other types of stone.

All types of turquoise are easily obtainable but care should be taken that what you are offered is the real stone and not a manufactured imitation. The imitations have become recently very popularly used in costume jewelry to mimic Native American art.

This is a highly protective stone that has been used for amulets for thousands of years. It is thought to activate the Third Eye during meditation and to enhance intuition. This crystal is said to change color as a warning of infidelity.

Zircon

Widely regarded as similar to the diamond, the zircon is thought to be a good crystal for coping with the stresses and strains of modern life. It has been valued for thousands of years.

Zircon comes in a number of colors—brown, blue, yellow, or colorless—and is known by several names. The brown zircon is known as the hyacinth or jacinth. Blue zircon (often heat-treated) is known as the Siam aquamarine and the colorless variety is called the Ceylon diamond.

All types of zircon are readily available at rock stores and jewelry shops, and are inexpensive.

Zircons are thought to be fortunate stones, making the wearer affable to others. Farmers once used this crystal to ensure good harvests. The brown variety is said to increase prosperity and protect travelers. It is also claimed to foretell changes in the weather. The stone glows brightly to foretell a sunny day and lose its shine if bad weather is coming.

Crystals
in Everyday
Life

9

B elief in the influence of crystals is spreading rapidly as more and more ways of using them are discovered. The stones possess healing powers and could be beneficial in many ways. Indeed, some enthusiasts allege that the earth itself is a giant crystal and that our physical bodies are composed of liquid crystals. Such claims remain unproven, but who is to know what will be revealed by further research? Certainly, crystals form an important part of 21st century technology, but here are some everyday uses you may not have considered.

Food and Drink

Crystals can be used to purify water. Simply drop a crystal into a glass of water and leave it overnight. Next morning, drink the water and you will almost certainly notice its clear, refreshing taste. This routine is said to clear the water of toxins. It is also claimed to enhance the flavor of fruit juice and other drinks and even to improve the taste of cheap wine.

> *Note: It is best to use clear quartz for this purpose. Other crystals may be used but be careful that they are not those that are damaged by immersion in liquid. Also, only use this method on water that is safe to drink and not on water that comes out of taps (faucets) in developing countries.*

You may care to try energizing your food with crystals. Simply place the stones on a working surface where you prepare food in the kitchen. The resulting dishes will be even more delicious than usual. Similarly, if you are feeling stressed, tired, and irritable when preparing food, it's a good idea to run a crystal round the rim of each serving dish before taking it to the table. This will eliminate the negative vibrations the food may have taken on during preparation. The freshness of fruit and vegetables will be extended if they are stored with crystals around them. Bread, cookies, and cakes benefit in the same way.

Most electronic equipment—such as microwave ovens— produce harmful emissions. As well as being physically unacceptable, these emissions can have a depressing effect. Counteract both risks by placing a crystal near each piece of equipment—not only in the kitchen, but beside television sets, near computers, and similar items in other rooms.

Incidentally, a piece of rose quartz will "calm" an irritable computer!

Indoor Plants

Flowers and plants also benefit from crystal power. Drop a small stone into a vase or place one on the surface of a plant pot. Amazing effects can be obtained by scattering crushed crystals over the compost in a pot. Some rock shops sell packets of this type of stone—so tiny they look like sparkling, multi-colored crumbs.

In the Garden

Crystals can be used to great effect in a garden. As an experiment, select a plant that is disappointing you and tuck a crystal into the ground at its base. Don't be surprised when its progress begins to outstrip everything else in the garden. It's cheaper—and more environmentally friendly—to scatter your garden with crystals than with chemical fertilizers.

Green stones are particularly appropriate for use in this way. Aventurine and malachite immediately spring to mind, particularly because both stones are associated with fertility. Herbs, though, respond better to hematite or smoky quartz. Place the stones on the earth near the base of the plants.

Crystals can also be used to improve the atmosphere of a garden. Try amethyst or tourmaline for relaxation, with clear quartz and jade for tranquility. These may be placed on the ground, in the seating area, or hung from the branches of trees.

Mundane Purposes

Hang crystals in your windows to catch the sun and produce rainbows of color on your walls. This is said to protect from negative vibrations, just as the atmosphere of any room is enhanced if crystals are placed in it.

A fretful baby can be soothed by placing a crystal beneath (not in) the crib. *Ensure that it is impossible for the child to actually touch (or swallow) the stone.*

Crystals can produce a calming, healing effect if placed near the bed in a sickroom and they will encourage the patient to sleep.

Give your pet crystal-charged water to drink—but remove the stone before you offer the water to the animal.

An increasing number of people are using crystals to ensure their safety while traveling. Some even place a small stone beneath the hood of the car as an insurance against engine troubles. Some also claim that this helps them to find a parking space.

Northern roads, much prone to icy conditions, are scattered with sand to prevent accidents—the composition of sand is largely fine grains of quartz!

Crystals placed at the entrance to your home provide a welcoming atmosphere for visitors.

These are just a few of the methods in which crystals can be used in everyday life. These may inspire you to experiment for yourself. Select a cleansed and charged stone of which you are particularly fond and program it to produce the results you require. For instance, place a crystal on the photograph of a friend with whom you have lost contact. It's probable that you will hear from that person soon. It's fun to experiment in this way, and you can produce some really astounding results. However, don't expect miracles from your crystals. As always— patience is a virtue much to be desired; the unique power of the crystal will make itself known.

Crystals and Feng Shui

The ancient Chinese tradition of Feng Shui is based on the positioning and balance of the qualities of *yin* and *yang* in the places where we live and work. This system has proved so effective that it is used by big business organizations throughout the world, as well as by ordinary people anxious to promote harmony in their homes. Crystal power works particularly well with Feng Shui, enhancing and balancing the flow of *chi* (the life force.) We offer here a few suggestions that will help you to gain the most benefit from both systems simply by placing certain crystals in the appropriate area of your home or office.

North

The north aspect of your home or office influences your career. The crystals needed here are carnelian, garnet, or ruby.

Northeast

In the northeast, the area of wisdom and enlightenment, smoky quartz, hematite, and black onyx will prove useful.

East

Family, children, and health are the areas with which the east is concerned. Suitable stones are lepidolite and snowflake obsidian.

Southeast

The southeast concerns wealth, property, and prosperity. Use lapis lazuli, sapphire, or turquoise to support this area.

South

In the south of your home or office, tiger's eye, topaz, and diamond will assist with fame and your reputation.

Southwest

Happy marriage, successful relationships, and peace are southwest concerns, with malachite and emerald being appropriate.

West

In the west, use pearl, moonstone, or white opal to enhance your creativity, fertility, and joy in life.

Northwest

Helpful people, travel, and new beginnings of any kind are the concerns of the northwest area, where clear quartz—in the form of a wand or cluster—will be especially effective.

A Crystal a Day

Some authorities consider that certain crystals are particularly helpful if worn or used on specific days of the week. You may want to experiment with this idea.

Day	Crystal
Sunday	Diamond or zircon
Monday	Moonstone, pearl, or malachite
Tuesday	Sapphire, ruby, or opal
Wednesday	Amethyst or kunzite
Thursday	Emerald, turquoise, or citrine
Friday	Alexandrite or cat's eye
Saturday	Labradorite, azurite, or lapis lazuli

Crystal
Correspondences

10

Crystal correspondences are everywhere—from birthstones, to zodiac signs, to special stones for anniversaries.

Birthstones

The use of crystals as birthstones is thought to have originated with the Biblical account of the breastplate of the High Priest Aaron (see page 14). The Bible tells us that this was embellished with twelve gemstones, each representing one of the twelve sons of Jacob, who later created the Twelve Tribes of Israel.

It is now believed that the powers of individual crystals can vary according to the time of the year. In consequence, the following list has developed. Anyone wearing a stone appropriate to his or her birth date should feel that it works as a personal talisman. If, for some reason, you are unable to resonate to one of your own "official" crystals, don't hesitate to select another that you feel is more appropriate. It will be equally effective. Both stones named have identical powers, so select the one you prefer and try to wear it always.

Month	Crystal
January	Garnet or rose quartz
February	Amethyst or onyx
March	Aquamarine or bloodstone
April	Diamond or clear quartz
May	Chrysoprase or emerald
June	Moonstone or pearl

July	Carnelian or ruby
August	Peridot or sardonyx
September	Lapis lazuli or sapphire
October	Opal or tourmaline
November	Tiger's eye or citrine
December	Turquoise or zircon

Crystals through the Zodiac

Some systems suggest stones for certain months, while astrological systems often select stones of a color that resonates with the zodiac sign. We have chosen two main stones for each sign, based on ancient principles and others that might help alleviate problems associated with your particular sign.

Aries

March 21–April 20

Diamond and bloodstone are, as a rule, associated with Aries and these stones will certainly help you to overcome the foolhardy impulses to which you are prone. If it's prosperity you're after, you can't do better than wear tiger's eye. Moonstone will assist when it comes to controlling your quick temper and help you to maintain a steady serenity. Rose quartz and garnet should be used to attract love to your life, allow you to give love to others, and dissolve your negative emotions.

Taurus

April 21—May 21

Emerald and sapphire are the crystals usually linked to Taurus and will help you to overcome your jealous nature. Amethyst will increase your creativity and also help to dispel any negative feelings you may have toward others. This crystal will also be useful if you are trying to come to terms with overeating. It won't actively make you lose weight, but it will help you to feel less ravenous. Tourmaline is the crystal to use as your magnet for money, but if you want to attract your true love, try wearing some green jade.

Gemini

May 22—June 21

Citrine and Alexandrite are the usual Gemini crystals. Worn together or separately they will help you to be more patient in your dealings with others. Green jasper will bring Geminis good fortune while blue lace agate will help you to focus more clearly on your objectives. Wearing this type of agate crystal will also make you more consistent and resolute when you have to make decisions. When it comes to finding your one true love, you'll find that pink tourmaline is the stone for you.

Cancer

June 22—July 23

Pearl and moss agate are the traditional crystals for Cancer and they will ensure that you are able to overcome your tendency to indifference and lethargy. You'll be surprised at the difference they will make to your energy levels. Both these crystals will also help you overcome any periods of depression you may experience. Lapis lazuli will keep you to balanced and aid your spiritual intuition. Sapphire and citrine will give you all the protection you need from those who tend to take advantage of your sensitive nature. Ruby and kunzite will enhance your love life while at the same time keeping your strong emotions in check.

Leo

July 24—August 23

Tiger's eye and amber are Leo's crystals. They will both help you to maintain your naturally courageous attitude in even the worst possible circumstances. On the rare occasions when you feel jaded and downhearted, choose a beautiful Herkimer diamond to boost your energy levels. This will also help you to control your tendency toward intolerance. Rose quartz and clear quartz will be most helpful as your love crystals. Wear them together for the greatest effect.

Virgo

August 24—September 23

Blue lace agate and sardonyx are the stones associated with Virgo. They will help you control your least desirable attribute—a tendency to be high-handed. Clear quartz will help you keep a clear mind and boost your imagination when the need arises. Citrine will overcome any sense of bitterness toward others and will also dispel any negative attitudes you may have. If love is proving elusive, wear rose quartz for speedy results.

Libra

September 24—October 23

Azurite and jade are Libran stones and will serve you well. They will drive out those feelings of insecurity that occasionally get you down. Another boost for you is to hold a Herkimer diamond when you are feeling despondent. It will swiftly drive away your blues. Wearing some malachite will help you to keep grounded. A crystal of aventurine encourages good luck and could well bring prosperity too. Green tourmaline is the crystal that will attract the love of your life.

Scorpio

October 24—November 22

Sodalite and opal are traditional Scorpio stones. Wearing either of them will make you more tolerant and less irritated by the foibles and follies of others. Carry some malachite in your purse or your pocket and you'll gain a more balanced attitude. A crystal of sodalite will help to guard against emotional upsets, while, at the same time, enabling you to express your emotions. Rhodocrosite is your talisman for finding true love.

Sagittarius

November 23—December 21

Topaz and carnelian are the most useful crystals for Sagittarius. Either one will help you to become much more considerate and predictable than you are at present. Clear quartz will ensure that you remain clear-headed and competent in anything you undertake. It will also boost your energy levels whenever needed. If you keep a piece of citrine on hand, good luck will stay with you wherever you go. If you're looking for love, ruby is the crystal to wear.

Capricorn

December 22—January 20

Garnet and smoky quartz are often Capricorn's favorite stones. They are also extremely beneficial in that they will dispel the intolerance and selfishness that are often Capricorn traits. Sodalite will develop and express your creativity to a degree you previously thought impossible. Add a tumbled bloodstone to your collection to ensure success in all your endeavors. A bed of clear quartz will make all your dreams come true. If you're still looking for love, then rose quartz is the crystal for you.

Aquarius

January 21—February 19

Aquamarine, garnet, and peridot are all crystals associated with Aquarius, and they can help you in different ways. Aquamarine will strengthen your resolve and show you that your life *does* have a purpose. Garnet will drive out any negativity that is destroying your confidence. Peridot, especially used with malachite, will act as your money magnet. Malachite also has a beneficial influence on business matters. If you've hit an unlucky streak, aventurine could bring about a change in your fortunes, but if you're looking for love, try wearing rhodochrosite.

Pisces

February 20—March 20

Moonstone and amethyst have always been associated with Pisces and are particularly efficient at dispelling nervous depression or anxiety. If your get-up-and-go has got up and gone, aquamarine will boost your energy levels. Malachite is guaranteed to bring you good fortune, particularly in financial dealings. And, if you wear tourmaline, true love will soon turn up.

Anniversaries

Traditionally, wedding anniversaries are marked by many elements, ranging from paper through steel to diamond. However, with the increasing popularity of crystals and gemstones, an alternative list has developed and this can be used for any kind of anniversary rather than just those associated with marriage.

Anniversary	Crystal
1.	Freshwater pearl
2.	Rose quartz
3.	Crystal (clear quartz)
4.	Blue topaz
5.	Sapphire
6.	Amethyst
7.	Onyx
8.	Tourmaline
9.	Lapis lazuli
10.	Blue sapphire

11.	Turquoise
12.	Jade
13.	Citrine
14.	Opal
15.	Garnet
16.	Peridot
17.	Carnelian
18.	Chrysoberyl
19.	Aquamarine
20.	Emerald
21.	Iolite
22.	Spinel
23.	Imperial topaz
24.	Tanzanite
25.	Green garnet (silver anniversary)
30.	Pearl
35.	Emerald
40.	Ruby
45.	Sapphire
50.	Golden topaz (golden anniversary)
55.	Alexandrite
60.	Diamond (diamond anniversary)
65.	Blue spinel
70.	Smoky quartz

Good Luck Charms

Crystals have been used as amulets and talismans for centuries. Many people carry a "lucky" crystal everywhere they go. If the idea appeals to you, you will first need to select the appropriate stone and then ensure that it is cleansed, purified, and programmed before you use it. If your luck begins to fail or if your crystal loses its sparkle, this is a sign to purify and program your stone again. For best results, carry it with you at all times. Don't allow other people to handle your crystal. In fact, don't even *tell* anyone else about it. When your friends marvel at your good fortune, simply smile and agree.

Here are the ten most powerful crystal luck-bringers.

Apache Tears

This is the star performer as an all-round good luck amulet. Carry it with you everywhere. Believe in it and wait for all your dreams to come true.

Aventurine

This heightens the precognitive abilities and is therefore an effective good luck charm in games of chance. Wear it at the casino, in the bingo hall, or when playing cards.

Citrine

This helps to create a favorable outcome in business negotiations. Carry one with you, but you could also keep a second stone in your desk at work.

Hematite

A large piece of hematite kept inside the front door or on a windowsill will bring good fortune to the house and those who live therein.

Jade

Jade brings friends and happy relationships, especially intimate ones. Give a piece to your partner.

Jasper

This provides all that you need. (Note the wording, because "all that you need" may be totally different from "all that you want.")

Malachite

This ensures faithfulness. Give your lover a piece of carved malachite as a totem.

Moss Agate

This brings good luck to the wearer in both business and private life. Only Apache Tears is stronger than moss agate.

Sodalite

This will bring the wearer good luck in financial dealings. Carry a piece when you visit your bank manager.

Turquoise

This is a healing stone that can be worn as a good luck talisman when you visit sick people.

Growing
Your Own
Crystals

11

Crystals that grow naturally are obviously the best and the most powerful but they can now be grown commercially. Diamonds, sapphires, and rubies can be produced in this way, though the process requires extremely high temperatures and pressures—not something you can do in your kitchen!

You can grow crystals quite easily at home without any special equipment, and there is no better introduction to crystals than to grow your own. You will, of course, be limited as to what you can grow, but this is an interesting undertaking and will fascinate children.

Minerals that dissolve in water are the only ones that can be used to grow crystals at home. These include alum, obtainable from most chemists, table salt, borax, sugar, and washing soda (**ed. note:** washing soda, available in stores, is *not* baking soda, although it can be made by heating baking soda. In addition: be sure that you don't get caustic soda—lye—by mistake.) The most spectacular result comes from copper sulphate, **but do be careful with this, particularly if children are involved, as it is poisonous.**

Take a large glass jug, mason jar, or vase—any sort of glass jar with a large top opening will do. Heat some water to near boiling point and drop in some of the substance from which you are going to make your crystals. Stir continually and keep adding the substance until no more will dissolve. This is called a saturated solution. Pour some of this into your glass container and leave it undisturbed and uncovered for several days. As the water cools and evaporates, crystals will start to form at the bottom of your jar. Leave these until you can see that they have stopped growing. From these small crystals choose the largest.

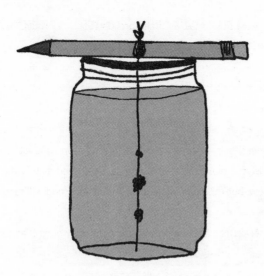

Make a fresh saturated solution of your substance. Put it aside to cool completely. This is important. If the solution is still warm, it will dissolve your large crystal.

Now tie a thread round your largest crystal and suspend it in your container, so that it not in contact with the jar in any way. This crystal will continue to grow, albeit slowly, for quite some time. When it stops growing, you can either remove it from the solution and carefully dry it or place it in a fresh saturated solution where it will continue to grow. You'll be surprised at the size of crystal that can be grown in this manner. Because it is home grown, it will be especially valuable and personal to you. Remember to dry it gently and carefully. Keep it well away from water and never try to wash it, as the crystal will immediately dissolve.

Try another practical guide in the
ORION PLAIN AND SIMPLE
series

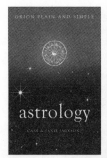

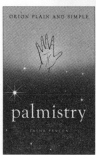

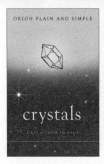